THE MIDAS TRAP

The Christianity Today Series

The Sexual Christian, by Tim Stafford

Tough Questions Christians Ask, David Neff, editor

The Blackboard Fumble, Ken Sidey, editor

What Every Christian Should Know,
by Jo H. Lewis and Gordon A. Palmer

Pentecostals from the Inside Out, Harold Smith, editor

Alien Gods on American Turf, by Terry C. Muck

The Midas Trap, David Neff, editor

The Crisis of Homosexuality, J. Isamu Yamamoto, editor

THE MIDAS TRAP

EDITED BY DAVID NEFF

VICTOR BOOKS®

A DIVISION OF SCRIPTURE PRESS PUBLICATIONS INC.
USA CANADA ENGLAND

Unless otherwise noted, all Scripture quotations are from the *Revised Standard Version,* © 1946, 1952, 1971, Division of Christian Education, National Council of Churches of Christ in the United States of America. Other quotations are from the *Holy Bible, New International Version* (NIV), © 1973, 1978, 1983 by International Bible Society. Used by permission of Zondervan Bible Publishers.

Cover illustration: Ronald Chironna

Library of Congress Cataloging-in-Publication Data

The Midas trap / edited by David Neff.
  p. cm.
    Includes text of the Oxford declaration on Christian faith and economics, issued jointly by more than 100 individuals attending the Oxford Conference on Christian Faith and Economics, Jan. 1990.
    ISBN 0-89693-286-9
    1. Wealth—Religious aspects—Christianity. 2. Steward-
    ship, Christian. 3. Christian giving. 4. Economics—
    Religious aspects—Christianity. I. Neff, David. II. Oxford
    declaration on Christian faith and economics. 1990.
  BR115.W4M53   1990
  261.8'5—dc20   90-36502
                                                      CIP

1 2 3 4 5 6 7 8 9 10 Printing/Year 94 93 92 91 90

CONTENTS

81457

THE REAL MONEY PROBLEM

David Neff

Recent press accounts have reported a controversy surrounding two houses of nuns committed to the ideal of poverty. Both houses belonged to the Poor Clares, an order founded by Clare of Assisi, a close friend of Saint Francis. She offered women a version of the jubilant, possession-free spirituality that had been pioneered by her eccentric soul mate.

The director of one house of Clares, through a corporation she herself controlled, was transforming a section of their historic convent into a luxury hotel. The other house had sold their convent as well as many of their art treasures to finance a villa in Southern France and a limousine to transport them there. Church officials were, to put it mildly, perplexed.

It is easy to snigger and tut-tut at these unconventional nuns. But

Christians from around the world are just as shocked when they get to know many American believers. The comparative wealth of middle-class Christians can seem eerily out of place in the face of poverty both here and abroad. And yet common sense tells us that the solution is not simply for us to trade in our business suits for tonsures and habits. The varied life situations into which believers are born or called demand different solutions.

Yet there are some common threads. Most American Christians, when asked about money problems, would say they don't have enough money—or perhaps that they don't manage what they have well enough. These believers are part of a culture that constantly reinforces these feelings—"The Great I Want" is what one author calls them. Thus most books about money either tell you how to make more (such as—we are not making this up—*How I Make One Thousand Dollars an Hour Talking on Radio Shows from My Home Phone in My Pajamas—& You Can, Too!*), or how to get by on less (such as *How to Live on Almost Nothing & Have Plenty*).

This book tries to do neither. For the real money problem is not a problem of quantity, but of liberty. When Jesus said, "You cannot serve both God and Mammon," he warned us about the potential power of wealth. (Wealth can hold us even when we don't hold it.) Being freed from bondage to wealth requires both an inner, attitudinal transformation and outer, behavioral adjustments. Anyone who tells you that you can have liberation without experiencing both kinds of changes also has some forbidden fruit for you to taste.

This book will stimulate you to consider the wisdom of Scripture on the subject of wealth. Scripture speaks two words about wealth: *blessing* and *beware*. Material comforts are good; they are gifts from God, and he intends that we enjoy them in abundance. But wealth is also a snare. It can trap us when there is great disparity between those who have and those who don't. It can ambush us when it offers us power over the lives of others. It can delude us when anxiety overwhelms trust. Like Scripture, this book speaks both words, but because of our time and our place, it says *beware* much more than it says *blessing*.

The Midas Trap had its origins in a meeting of Scripture scholars. In November 1988, while nearly 5,000 persons swarmed to the annual meeting of the American Academy of Religion and the

Society of Biblical Literature, a dozen evangelical scholars took time for a spirited discussion of the issues surrounding the Bible and wealth. Several of those subsequently contributed articles to the Christianity Today Institute, "Rich Wisdom: New Testament Teachings on Wealth" (CHRISTIANITY TODAY, May 12, 1989, pp. 27–40). Those authors represent a variety of different ethical approaches within the stream of orthodox Protestantism. In this book, we have done little to minimize the tensions among them. As followers of Christ, we have much to struggle with here.

Some of those original essays are augmented here, and other authors have supplemented the original material with chapters about related concerns—ranging from the benevolence of women in the history of the church to the spiritual implications of the Sabbath for our relations to wealth.

Many thanks are due our authors. An extra measure of recognition is due to J. Isamu Yamamoto, tireless editor of the Christianity Today book series, and to Marty L. White, CHRISTIANITY TODAY's editorial coordinator, who not only directed the intricate dance of manuscripts, galleys, and corrections that make up the complex choreography of a multi-author work, but also assisted in developing Appendix 2. Errors in judgment or accuracy are, of course, entirely my responsibility.

Chapter 1

A TYRANNY OF STEWARDSHIP

J. Isamu Yamamoto

I have never taken off my clothes to sleep with my money, but that is what Trina McTeague did. She was a fictional character, described in Frank Norris's *McTeague*. I am flesh, blood, hair, and bone. But Trina and I have both been seduced by Mammon.

In the novel *McTeague*, avarice is the ruling passion of the protagonist and his wife. It tells the story of the moral degeneration of a man under economic pressures, but the portrait of McTeague's wife, Trina, is what haunts our imagination.

After being beaten, robbed, and deserted by McTeague, Trina's love for money overcomes her sorrow and becomes her dominant passion, brooding in her heart, driving out every other natural affection.

"She had her money," wrote Norris, "that was the main thing.

Her passion for it excluded every other sentiment. . . . Not a day passed that Trina did not have it out where she could see and touch it. One evening she had even spread all the gold pieces between the sheets, and had then gone to bed, stripping herself, and had slept all night upon the money, taking a strange and ecstatic pleasure in the touch of the smooth flat pieces the length of her entire body."

Stripped naked, Trina's soul is bared to us, and we see a person clutching, not an idol or a fetish, but a faceless doll in the form of coins. Trina yearns for money, not because she desires wealth, power, or even financial security, but because she desperately needs to love—like a child who clings to her doll before she drifts to sleep alone; and in money, she embraces a lover who will not abuse and abandon her.

Trina is not alone in her infatuation with money. Many of us have been seduced by it. For some, wealth is an idol on whose altar we sacrifice the futile years of seeking security; for others, it fuels the engines of power and prestige. But money is never inert, a mere means; a surcharge of the heart must always be paid. For me this passion was a yearning for affluence—a yearning that would gradually distort my values.

In the counting house

During the fifties, I spent many a lonely childhood hour counting and recounting the few coins that dribbled my way. For many people, the fifties are "the good old days" of family togetherness and growing suburban affluence. But for many Japanese-Americans in California, those times were not exactly "happy days." Living in mostly Anglo neighborhoods as a Japanese-American kid, I was constantly reminded that I was the "enemy." Afraid to make friends with people, I formed an attachment to money.

My earliest memories are of living in a two-room house—my parents sleeping in one room, my brother and I sleeping in the other, which served as the functions of kitchen, living room, and every other need. I recall my father laboring in the cherry orchards and my mother rubbing our clothes on a second-hand washboard; and I, at age five, would be calculating how many Coke bottles I could find and convert into pennies, coins to be rolled and secreted in my cigar-box cache.

After my father took up landscape gardening, we moved into a two-bedroom house in suburbia. I was in third grade. Although our move to the suburbs was a step up the social ladder, I still yearned for the affluence I constantly saw on television. I wanted to live in a big house like Beaver Cleaver, wear expensive clothes like Ricky Nelson. And so I stuffed rolls of dimes and nickels under piles of comic books and baseball cards.

On Saturday mornings I would grudgingly crawl out of bed at 4:30. Thirty minutes later, I would be bouncing up and down in my dad's old, loose-jointed truck. By the time we arrived on the grounds of the paper plant he cared for, I would be half conscious of the bright stars in the sky and the chill wind slapping my face. For the next several hours, I would drag an endless water hose from juniper to juniper. This routine lasted several years and taught me the meaning of monotony.

My one consolation: I was paid two or three dollars a week, a goodly amount thirty years ago. Each week, I would deposit my earnings in the bank and feel the warm pleasure of marking the new total in my passbook. My parents encouraged my thrift because, like many Japanese-American parents, they strongly wanted me to attend college so I could secure a good job.

A person can contemplate a great deal while watching water arc from one's finger to the sunken earth. As I watered the junipers, I pondered two things. One was my money, increasing in the bank at 3 percent interest. The mental calculations of how much it would grow in a year absorbed me. In one year, this amount; in two years, that amount; in three years, so much more; and on and on like the water filling one plant basin after another. Eventually my mind would rest on the year there would be enough for me to live off part of the interest, while the sum would continue to increase.

The other thing that occupied my mind was the ideal girl. She would be someone who would waltz into my life like Ginger Rogers and fulfill my dreams: a sweet, adoring, lovely girl who would fall deeply and instantly in love with *me*. But in my adolescence, no girl even stumbled into my life. I was too different, too alien, to be acknowledged. When I accepted Christ into my life at age twenty, however, I changed and so did my life. Soon, thereafter, Susan entered my life and fell in love with me as I did with her.

Desperately seeking Susan

But as much as God changes us when he embraces us, there are still some weeds that need to be ripped out of us. One was my passion for money—not necessarily enough to be lavish, like a Gatsby or a Hearst, but enough to be as comfortable as the Andersons on "Father Knows Best." By this time, I was in college, sadly watching my savings dwindle. Each cent had to be spent carefully and wisely if I were to avoid the thing I feared the most—debt. And so I spent very little on Susan. She never complained, because money did not abide in her mind as it did in mine. But many things she wanted us to do—things we should have done—we never did: going out to dinner or the theater—simple, but refreshing memories that would have carried us through the desert times of our relationship.

In my senior year, my parents, Susan, and I drove together to Reno, Nevada, where a justice of the peace married my brother and his fiancée. After the wedding ceremony, Susan and I stood idly in a casino lobby while a one-armed bandit held my father captive. On a whim, I slipped a nickel into a nearby slot machine. A cherry appeared, and three nickels dashed into a pot before me. I turned to Susan, and she gave me a smile. I quickly shoved one of the nickels back into the machine. This time the machine was silent. *Why not?* I thought, as I pushed another nickel into the maw of the machine and pulled the arm. One by one three *Jackpots* lined up across the middle. A bell clamored, and Susan laughed and clasped her hands as a thousand nickels filled the bin.

On the way home, she talked excitedly about different things we could do with the fifty dollars—we could go bowling or see *A Chorus Line* in the city. While she chattered, I nodded and thought about different things I could buy for her with the jackpot money—Capezio shoes or a bracelet. But my thoughts turned to the books I needed to purchase for my last semester, and I convinced myself that this money was God's way of helping me through college.

We never did the things she talked about, nor did I buy her the things I dreamt of. I never told her what I planned to do with the money. Nor did she ask me. She simply ceased to ask me when we could go bowling. I knew she was disappointed, but I could not straighten my bent values, fearfully grasping at little signs of security as the one I loved slipped away. And as the weeks passed by,

the desert times grew longer as I anxiously pondered my professional future.

Susan had "polished eyes" and a "toothpaste smile"—as I often
told her. But one day at my parents' home, a sadness clouded her
features as she left. She desperately wanted my affection, but I was
too worried about getting a teaching job after college to give her an
intimate smile or a friendly touch. Hurting and distracted, she did
not notice a neighbor's car behind hers. She crunched into his car,
remarkably not damaging her Pinto, but giving his car an obvious
dent. She was devastated. Susan's mother had forbidden her to see
me because of my race, and since the insurance was in her mother's
name, our secret would become known. Her mother would discover
the accident had occurred on forbidden territory, and she would
know we were still going together.

I consoled Susan, telling her I would deal with the neighbor
privately. He agreed to a cash settlement without insurance involvement. She went home partly appeased, but anxious about the money
it would cost her. Later the neighbor told me his bumper would cost
a couple of hundred dollars to replace.

This was when I read *McTeague*. The image of Trina's naked
embrace of money pricked my conscience. Although the circumstances were different, money had twisted her values as it had mine.
When McTeague returned, starving, Trina refused to give him a
crumb. Her love for him had died. I, too, had withheld what I had
from my love, but for the security of my academic future.

But now, compared to Susan, English textbooks seemed like
wastepaper. I used the jackpot money and my savings to pay for
most of the car repair. I wanted to lessen Susan's worries, and I
wanted to show her she meant much more to me than Mammon. But
I never told her the true cost of the bumper. I gave her a much lower
figure, which she gradually paid to the neighbor. Meanwhile, I paid
a price for my miserly inclinations. Susan had wanted very deeply to
have a loving husband, and within two years her dream was
fulfilled. She was married—to another man.

Steward and servant
When the Canaanite woman implored Jesus to deliver her demon-
possessed daughter, Jesus initially refused—probably to make a

point. He said he was sent for only the house of Israel. But she persisted in seeking his mercy, crying that even dogs receive crumbs. He healed her daughter because people are of much greater value than any idea.

How much more than crumbs we give to those in need depends on how much more people are of value to us than is Mammon and its promises of security or comfort or power. Had anyone asked me, I would have sworn Susan meant a great deal more to me than money. But I had failed to see the subtle lies I had told myself. I believed I was being a good steward with my money. But I was so possessed by "stewardship" that I forgot I was to be a servant as well. Money has its place, but it should never displace people.

My yearning for affluence began to wane, but I don't know whether that passion for money expired because I spent the jackpot for the right reason, because I was haunted by the image of Trina McTeague, or because I was shocked by the loss of Susan's love. I only know that whenever Mammon begins to make material things seem to take on a life of their own, I need to look closely at my values in the same way Jesus valued the Canaanite woman and her daughter.

Mammon has power to lure any heart, save that whose affection is fully given to Christ.

Chapter 2

THE HARD SAYINGS OF JESUS

Thomas Schmidt

Most North American Christians try carefully to follow the teachings of Jesus, but when his words deal with the nature and use of wealth, we tend to look away from him rather than toward him for ways to explain away these passages. We look longingly to the wealthy patriarchs and kings in the Old Testament; we quote business advice from the Book of Proverbs; we scour the Gospels for rich people who do not get condemned; or we infer generously from Paul's relative silence on the subject. In short, we interpret the plain, disturbing teaching of Jesus in the light of everything else instead of interpreting everything else in the light of Jesus' teaching.

Believers have always struggled with the harsh words of Jesus about wealth, but it was probably in Puritan England that the seeds of today's prosperity theology were sown. So many earnestly pious people were prospering that it was difficult not to see wealth as a reward for righteousness. Wisely, they tempered this deduction by stressing such virtues as simplicity, charity, modesty, and personal discipline. Later, John Wesley pushed the sensible formula "Make all you can, save all you can, give all you can." More recently, Christians appear to have concluded that two out of three is not bad.

But what of the teaching of Jesus on wealth? Is it only directed toward rich young rulers and perhaps toward the disciples for the period of his public ministry? Certainly not. The Gospels were written 30 to 40 years after Jesus' public ministry not merely to inform about the past, but also to instruct the readers of that and all subsequent generations. Jesus goes as far as to say that only those who obey his words will enter the kingdom (Matt. 7:21–27). Which of his words would he say were no longer relevant a generation (or two millennia) later? The principles behind those words clearly apply in the modern world. Let us consider some of the words themselves.

The command to sell all

As a familiar story repeated in three of the Gospels (Matt. 19:16–30; Mark 10:17–31; Luke 18:18–30), the account of the rich young ruler is a good place to begin. Jesus responds to the man's question about eternal life by telling him to sell all his possessions, give to the poor, and follow Jesus. The man refuses. Jesus goes on to explain how difficult it is for rich people to get into heaven. If one wonders whether Jesus meant "very difficult" or "impossible," one need only attempt to insert a camel through the eye of a needle. Well-meaning attempts to shrink the camel (by the claim that Jesus said "cable" rather than "camel") or to enlarge the needle (by the medieval legend that there was a small gate in the wall of ancient Jerusalem called "the needle's eye") are creative, but desperate.

The disciples react in amazement to such a rigorous demand, and Jesus responds that it is indeed impossible without God. This is clearly not a statement that the rich man will be saved anyway because God will forgive him. Such an explanation would make Jesus' teaching up to that point meaningless. It is obvious that the disciples get the point, because they respond with a question about the adequacy of their own "leaving all." Jesus affirms this response and adds that everyone who acts the same way will get the same reward. He does not digress into a discussion of God's grace in spite of our disobedience; he speaks of our action, which must appropriate God's power.

Another important passage is Luke 14:25–33, which ends with the disturbing statement, "So therefore, no one of you can be my disciple who does not give up all his possessions" (NASB). It is not possible to reduce the impact of this command by spiritualizing it. Jesus is not commanding followers merely to give up an ambiguous "everything" (an interpretation that, in practice, usually means "nothing"). The word for possessions here is used elsewhere in the New Testament only for material goods (e.g., Matt. 19:21; Luke 12:33). Nor does he say that one must be merely "willing" to give up all; the verb is used elsewhere in the New Testament only for actual abandonment (e.g., Mark 6:46; Acts 18:18).

There is a tendency to spiritualize the possession of wealth by claiming that "in my heart I have given it all to God." This may follow from the justifiable position that one's attitudes and motives matter as much to God as one's actions. But Jesus, in contrasting God and wealth, does not allow this option of believing one way and acting another. One or the other, God or wealth, is one's "employer" (Matt. 6:24; Luke 16:13), and the one that is not served is hated. (The term *hatred* is intended to stress further the separation between God and material wealth. It is used similarly in Luke 14:26, 33 to show that believers must never place family or possessions on the same plane as Christ.) If his language is strong, it is because he knows "Where your treasure is, there will your heart be also" (Matt. 6:21). One's conduct with money *reveals* the state of the heart.

There are numerous other troubling passages. Jesus concludes the parable of the rich fool in Luke 12:21 with the warning against placing wealth above being "rich toward God." Later in the same chapter he commands his disciples to apply this by selling possessions and giving to the poor (12:33). Luke 16:9 is a rather obscure command that believers should "make friends for yourselves by means of the unrighteous mammon, so that when it fails they may receive you into the eternal habitations." This command could be paraphrased to say, "Give away your possessions so that when you die God will give you eternal reward."

In the story of the rich man and Lazarus (Luke 16:19–31), the rich man is guilty for neglecting the poor man at his gate, and it seems that his comfortable life "clothed in purple and fine linen" may have contributed to his punishment. When Jesus explains the parable of the sower (Mark 4:14–20), he describes people whose initial response to the truth is destroyed by "the cares of this world, and the deceitfulness of riches, and the lusts of other things." The second phrase is particularly strong because it describes wealth as *deceitful.* Is this too harsh? Jesus is even more harsh on at least one occasion. When the money-loving Pharisees scoff at Jesus' teaching about choosing between God and wealth (Luke 16:10–14), Jesus responds that "what is exalted among men is an abomination in the sight of God." Jesus is not attacking pride here—no one exalts pride—but rather the *cause* of pride: the possession of money. The word *abomination* could not be stronger; it is used elsewhere of idolatry (e.g., see Ezra 9:11; Rom. 2:22).

In all of these passages, Jesus clearly condemns the possession of wealth.

Exceptions in the Gospels?

Since the composite effect of these passages can be devastating, we try to lessen their impact. There are several ways to do this. One is to point to examples of rich believers in the Gospels who are not condemned. Zacchaeus (Luke 19:1–10) is cited most often. Jesus announces the salvation of this man after he pledges, "Half of my goods I give to the poor; and if I have defrauded any one of anything, I restore it fourfold." It is a mistake to read this as a justification for retaining half of one's wealth (but how many do even that much?). Zacchaeus retains half his wealth not in order to sustain a comfortable lifestyle, but in order to channel his giving to the appropriate sources. His former victims would hardly be impressed by the news that he had given their money to the poor. His fourfold restitution would quickly deplete his resources. Zacchaeus, then, is not an example of acceptable wealth but a contrast to the rich man in the previous chapter who would not give away his wealth.

Some have pointed to Luke 22:35–36—where Jesus tells his disciples they should now carry purses, bags, and swords—to counter his previous teaching about wealth. If so, it is strange to find such a great quantity of teaching earlier in the Gospel, and addressed specifically to *disciples* at that. What is far more likely is that this passage describes the specific urgent situation in the garden where Jesus is "reckoned with transgressors" (22:27). The passage is difficult to understand, but there is not ample reason to consider it an exception to the teaching about possessions elsewhere in the Gospels.

The disturbing truth is that Matthew, Mark, and Luke present a consistently negative picture of wealth. There simply are no significant exceptions, and whatever straws one attempts to grasp are overwhelmed by the repeated and clear statements directed by Jesus to people who would follow him. The possession of wealth creates a false sense of security, the opposite of that complete dependence on God without which no one will be saved. The texts do not give a precise definition of wealth other than to suggest that any material possession has the potential to become valued more highly than God (Matt. 6:19–20; Mark 12:44). But even with a less radical definition of wealth, almost every North American Christian will feel the sting of these harsh words.

What to do?
Every time Jesus offers an opinion about riches, it is negative. Every time he teaches about the use of wealth, he counsels disciples to give it away. For people who take the Bible seriously, and who take Jesus most seriously of all, how seriously should we respond to these teachings about wealth? It may be time for more believers to consider the most obvious and least comfortable option: to obey them—to conform our lives to the commands of our Lord rather than the other way around.

What would it mean if we at least moved in the direction of Jesus' words? For one thing, it would put us in closer contact with Christians through the ages who have made a significant impact on the world around them. Unlike the Puritans, for example, modern believers appear to be immune to a sense of shame. Not only the more dramatic demands of discipleship, but even most of the little taboos that once marked us off from nonbelievers are now optional. The result is a moral vacuum, an absence of pressure to "witness" by our behavior in specific areas. The proper use of wealth could be an enormously influential area of witness for believers, such that the world·might begin to see this Christianity responding rather than contributing to the sin of materialism.

Of course, such a commitment involves a risk. What will God do with us when we fall short of perfect obedience, as most of us will in this and other areas? If we refuse to water down the demand but then fail to do the good thing that we could do, are we making a mockery of God's mercy? These are key questions that may suggest why we are tempted to water down the commands in the first place. Why bother to heed these teachings on wealth if in the end we fail to live up to them?

The answer lies in maintaining a continual tension, treading a razor-edge line between obedience and mercy. The demands of Jesus are there to be met. The forgiveness of Jesus is there to meet our failure. The Cross covers precisely the distance, for each of us, between what we attain and what God demands—between our striving and our arriving.

But if we refuse to move we deny the need for forgiveness, and that destroys the tension. We must hold on just as tenaciously to the words of Jesus about obedience as we do to the words of Paul about grace.

Obedience will inevitably seem to be much further away than grace, but to stand still because the goal is distant is to miss the point that discipleship is a journey. We begin at different points and we move at different rates, and that should prevent us from measuring one another's progress. But the biblical message is clear enough about the destination.

How much of our wealth should we give away? More.

Chapter 3

ENJOYING CREATION— WITHIN LIMITS

Raymond C. Van Leeuwen

Everything created by God is good, and nothing is to be rejected if it is received with thanksgiving; for it is hallowed *by the word of God and prayer. (1 Tim. 4:4–5, RSV modified)*

T he Bible calls the splendid world that came from God's hand very good, but the Bible also forbids us to idolize the world's goods or let them steal our hearts. God created the cosmos as the theater of his glory, and man and woman as his royal image on its stage. From the monarch butterfly to the great blue whale, from the quark to the spiral nebula, the majesty and wonder of God's creation show forth his boundless wealth and wisdom. In the holy temple of creation, God deigned to dwell with Adam and Eve, to walk with them in the cool of the day. But for all its goodness, creation is not God, nor should our love for any created good displace our love for him. From the very beginning, God set limits to our earthly loves but bade us love him boundlessly with heart and soul and strength.

We are not to love the world and its goods in the place of God. Yet, God shows us his love by means of this world. His earth feeds us, clothes us, and offers us an abundance of joys: the rising upward of a lark at dawn, the pulsing air that makes organ music sound, the holy communion of bodies that makes married love a mirror of Christ and his church (Eph. 5:21–33[1]). Even God's love in Christ is possible only because "the word became *flesh* and dwelt among us," an earthling whose blood is our atonement. It is by means of this world that we show our proper love for God, for our neighbor, and for ourselves. This world with its goods, including our bodies (Rom. 12:1–2), is all we have to express our faith, hope, and love. What we do with this world and its wealth matters.

God created the world for *shalom*, for "peace and prosperity." *Shalom* (and its companion, *righteousness)* implies harmony: "God's in his heaven and all's right with the world"; every man is "under his vine and fig tree." *Shalom* means peace between God and humankind, among tribes and nations, among generations and neighbors, spouses and families. The property of the defenseless, of the widow and orphan, is respected (Prov. 15:25; 22:28; 23:10; Deut. 19:14). Eve's children are at home in the world and with one another. *Shalom* also means that people are in harmony with the earth, in tune with "the nature of things." The prosperity of the sons of Adam is not purchased by the rape of creation.

Thus we cannot talk about wealth and poverty without considering God's will for creation. Wealth is *rooted* in the creation with its God-given order and limits. Creation includes not only what we moderns call "nature," but also "culture" and "society." Scripture suggests the overarching unity of nature and society by placing both under the umbrella of *righteousness*. In fact, the Swiss scholar H. H. Schmid has summed up Old Testament righteousness as "world-order," a world (including nature and society) ordered the way God intended it to be.[2]

In the New Testament, Christ came to restore the kingdom and righteousness of God on this earth. This combination is what Jesus told his followers to seek *first* (Matt. 6:33). And we Christians still "wait for new heavens and a new earth in which righteousness dwells" (2 Pet. 3:13). Righteousness is something built into the fabric of creation itself: the heavens show it and humans need to live by it. Psalm 50:6 states, "The *heavens* declare his righteousness, for God himself is judge!"

Nor can we discuss wealth as a matter of individual morality, apart from society. Wealth is not simply the product of individuals. Rather, it is the product of a vast interconnected network of human activity that uses or abuses God's creation. Wealth has a social, cultural dimension. Hence, we must first discuss wealth in terms of God's order for the natural realm (the *source* of all wealth), and second, in terms of God's order for society.

The earth and wealth

The first biblical principle concerning wealth is this:

> The earth is the Lord's and the fullness thereof, the world and those who dwell therein. (Ps. 24:1)

> Every beast of the forest is mine,
> the cattle on a thousand hills.
> I know all the birds of the air,
> and all that moves in the field is mine. (Ps. 50:10–11)

> The land shall not be sold in perpetuity, *for the land is mine;*
> for you are strangers and sojourners with me. (Lev. 25:23; cf.
> Heb. 11:13; 1 Pet. 2:11)

In biblical Hebrew, the word for "earth" and "land" is the same: *'erets*. This world and all things in it belong totally to God and to Christ (Col. 1:15–20; Rom. 11:36). We are only tenant farmers, so to speak, on God's property. All we claim as "ours" is really his. Yet God "gives" the earth to humans, his image bearers, so that they may be its caretakers and royal stewards (Gen. 1:26–28; Ps. 8). These passages often have been misunderstood to mean that humans could exploit the earth without limits to suit their own shortsighted desires. But biblical "ruling" or "dominion" always means *author-*

ity and power for the well-being of the subjects. A king is to rule as a *servant* of his subjects. "If you will be a servant to this people today and serve them, ... then they will be your servants forever," so counseled the wise elders to Rehoboam (1 Kings 12:7). And Jesus put it this way:

> You know that those who are supposed to rule over the Gentiles lord it over them, and their great men exercise authority [and power][3] over them. But it shall not be so among you; but whoever would be great among you must be your servant, and whoever would be first among you must be slave of all. For the Son of man also came not to be served but to serve, and to give his life as a ransom for many. (Mark 10:42b–45)

God gives to Abraham and his descendants the promise of land. And the apostle Paul understands that to mean the entire earth! "The promise to Abraham and his descendants, that they should inherit the world, did not come through the law but through the righteousness of faith" (Rom. 4:13). In the New Testament, the descendants of Abraham are those who by faith belong to Christ, the promised "offspring" of Abraham (Gal. 3:18). Jesus himself put the same promise in different language, "Blessed are the meek, for they shall inherit the earth" (Matt. 5:5).

The earth, or land, is the foundational gift of God to humans. Land is the basis of all wealth. He who has land has wealth. Land, the earth, provides us with the raw material for life itself. Without land there can be no worship, no praise of God, no obedience in life and work. Without land there is no life. The land is room to live; it provides beauty and joy; it brings forth food to eat and metal for the arts of civilization. God gave Israel

> a good land, a land of brooks of water, of fountains and springs, flowing forth in valleys and hills, a land of wheat and barley, of vines and fig trees and pomegranates, a land of olive trees and honey, a land in which you will eat bread without scarcity, in which you will lack nothing, a land whose stones are iron, and out of whose hills you can dig copper. And you shall eat and be full, and you shall bless the

LORD your God for the good land he has given you. (Deut. 8:7–10)

When Israel entered the promised land, God gave to each tribe, clan, and family its allotted portion (Josh. 13–21). God's will was that each family have the land necessary to provide at least the basics for life (Deut. 15:4). To insure the fair distribution of land from generation to generation, the law required that the portions of land stay within families (Lev. 25; Deut. 15; 1 Kings 21). If a portion was sold, it would return to its family in the year of jubilee, about once every generation. Gordon Wenham, in his fine commentary, *The Book of Leviticus*, writes,

> The jubilee was intended to prevent the accumulation of the wealth of the nation in the hands of a very few. Every Israelite had an inalienable right to his family land and to his freedom. (p. 323)

Thus a basic purpose of this law was to prevent poverty (Deut. 15:4). When the law of jubilee was ignored, God spoke judgment against the wealthy through his prophets:

> Woe to those who join house to house,
>   who add field to field,
> until there is no more room,
>   and you are made to dwell alone. (Isa. 5:8; see 5:1–7)

> They covet fields, and seize them;
>   and houses, and take them away;
> they oppress a man and his house,
>   a man and his inheritance. (Mic. 2:2)

Today our cultural situation is greatly changed from that of ancient Israel. But the biblical *principles* of justice and righteousness concerning the land, wealth, and poverty still hold. Wenham sums up one implication of jubilee for the modern world in this way:

> The biblical law is opposed equally to the monopolistic tendencies of unbridled capitalism and thorough-going communism, where all property is in state hands. (p. 323)

God requires justice and righteousness with regard to land and wealth. He especially expects it of those who know him and his Word. Both Isaiah and Jesus use the parable of the vineyard to represent Israel's and our duty to use the earth and its riches to produce fruits of justice and righteousness (Isa. 5:1–12; Matt. 21:33–46; cf. 23:23; Luke 11:42).

The blessings that go with obedience to biblical principles of justice and righteousness still can be obtained today, whether or not people recognize them as "biblical." And disobedience to these principles still leads to loss of blessing. Holly Brough writes in a recent issue of *World Watch* magazine that

> East Asian history shows that any development package will have trouble surmounting the odds in the Philippines unless it starts by redistributing the nation's agricultural land. It's a little known fact that the "miracle" nations of Japan, South Korea and Taiwan based their economic growth on land reforms pushed through in the tumultuous post-war years. Feudal estates were dismantled to form small, owner-operated farms, alleviating rural poverty and creating stronger and more equitable local economies.
>
> The Philippines cannot hope to skip this step on its path out of developing-nation status.[4]

At the time this book is being written (January 1990), it appears that President Aquino's political problems are partly related to her inability to fulfill her promises for land reform. The rich appear unwilling to practice the principle of "Jubilee,"[5] and the poor and hungry are thus tempted by the false gospel of Marxism.

Wealth and the limits of creation

God, however, does not only require that humans share the riches of the earth in a just and righteous way, but he has also so designed the world that it surrenders its wealth, from generation to generation, only to those who respect its order and limits. Humans need to listen to creation, to learn from it, and to live in harmony with its laws. To repeat: *Shalom* also means that people are in harmony with the earth, in tune with "the nature of things."

Isaiah says that *God* is teaching the farmer even as he learns from "hands-on" experience and traditional wisdom how to treat the earth and its crops (28:23–29). In a beautiful memoir called " 'A Handful of Mud': A Personal History of My Love for the Soil," veteran missionary doctor Paul Brand shows that a wise, earth-taught farmer preserves the topsoil for hundreds of generations to come.[6] Where there is *shalom*, the riches of creation—mineral, vegetable, animal, and cultural—and the wealth of nations are not at war with one another. Short-lived prosperity is not purchased by the rape or poisoning of creation. The good land God gave to the fathers is handed down, whole and wholesome, to sons and daughters, generation after generation.[7]

Israel knew that humans must *listen* to the wisdom that God has hidden in creation. God's creatures themselves are to *teach* us (Job 12:7–10; Ps. 19; Prov. 8; Rom. 1:18–20).[8] The prophets sometimes lament that animals know God's creation ordinances better than his disobedient people:

> Even the stork in the heavens knows her times;
> and the turtledove, swallow, and crane
>   keep the time of their coming;
> but my people know not the ordinance of the LORD.
> "How can you say, 'We are wise,
>   and the law of the LORD is with us?' "
> (Jer. 8:7–8a; see Isa. 1:3–17)

Creation, the Fall, and the violation of limits

For Adam and Eve, the continued experience of Creation's goodness depended on their submission to the order that God established in the beginning. In Genesis 1, God set limits for all his creatures by separations and distinctions: light from dark, waters from waters, earth from water. Each plant and animal was created "according to its kind." The church father Irenaeus rightly took this phrase, seen in the larger context of Scripture, to mean that "to the whole world [God] has given laws, that each one keep to his place and overstep not the bound laid down by God, each accomplishing the work marked out for him." In the Bible, such bounds are most powerfully represented by God's limiting command to the sea: "Thus far shall you come, and no farther, and here shall your proud waves be stayed" (Job 38:11; cf. Prov. 8:29; Ps. 104:8–9, NIV).

The mysterious thing is that only humans can overstep the bounds laid down by God (Jer. 5:22–29). By an act of trespass, humans violate their creaturely limits and mangle the good by ripping it from its proper place. The story of the Fall illustrates this concretely. Eve was tempted by good. God had created nothing bad or evil of itself. "The woman saw that the tree was good. . . ." In Hebrew this line exactly imitates the glad refrain of Genesis 1, "And God saw that it was good."

But of all the good trees, God had placed one off limits. Seduced by the serpent, Eve tasted the fruit that did not belong to her. Sin, we might say, is an attempt to displace God as the Creator by redrawing the limits of creation to suit our will rather than his. So, too, a married man may be tempted, not by evil per se, but by the beauty and grace of his neighbor's wife. She may be very good, but she is not good for him. For when God created marriage, he sharply etched the exclusive channels in which sexual love may flow (Prov. 5:15–19).

I know someone who would love to eat three pounds of Dutch chocolates a day and not pay the penalty. Sin wants freedom from limits, forbidden acts without consequences. Sin wants something good, some luxury, some joy, some thrill or power or intimacy. But it wants that good at the expense of reality. The sinner seeks to expand his little kingdom at the cost of the order and total goodness of God's righteous kingdom.

But the Creator is not mocked. The order and limits of his creation cannot be forever violated with impunity. Eventually we reap what we sow. This law of creation holds true in the social and moral realms. Americans still like to believe that "There's more where that came from!" and "The sky's the limit!" (meaning there are no limits). But our failure to respect the limits of creation and to preserve the earth for our children's children will someday bear its unhappy fruit. Sooner or later, in the timing of God's justice, social, political, economic, and ecological transgressions lead to bitter suffering and finally death. When humans try to play creator, to redraw the boundaries; when we trespass the limits; we die a little—or a lot, like fish out of water. This tragedy is true not only

for individuals, but for nations and cultures (Dan. 4:26–27).
Psalm 9 pictures it this way:

> The nations have sunk in the pit which they made;
> in the net which they hid has their own foot been caught.
> The LORD has made himself known, he has executed judgment;
> the wicked are snared in the work of their own hands.
> (vv. 15–16; cf. 7:14–16)

Here we see God's judgment in the natural consequences of human actions. The results are ordinary, even predictable. God respects the integrity of his own handiwork! Therefore, those who do not live in tune with reality inevitably suffer. The drunkard's liver is ruined because he has violated God's order for the body. *Furthermore, what Psalm 9 makes clear is that the creational law of acts and consequences also applies to nations and societies as they live out their deepest moral and spiritual values.*

It may be, however, that sinners themselves do not appear to suffer. But it is obvious that others do. For every happy thief, there is a violated victim; for every successful tyrant, there are suffering citizens; and for every prosperous polluter, there are deformed babies.

Perhaps an American illustration of this biblical law of cause and effect, of "acts and consequences," is in order. Let us take an example from business, an instance where "the maximization of profits" exceeded not only the limits of morality (as it too often does), but of legality. In the decades of the thirties and forties, several big and famous American corporations banded together in a criminal conspiracy to eliminate their competition and expand their markets. Jonathan Kwitny tells the story well in "The Great Transportation Conspiracy" (*Harper's*, February 1981).

General Motors, Standard Oil of California, Firestone Tire, Phillips Petroleum, and others set up dummy corporations for the purpose of buying up streetcar companies in many American cities. Once bought, entire electric streetcar systems were dismantled and replaced with less popular buses. "What followed was the destruction of mass transit; the country became almost totally reliant on the private automobile, with its necessary consumption of foreign oil," writes Kwitny. The mass advent of the car radically changed the landscape and atmosphere of many cities. In any case, more cars, tires, gas, and buses were sold.

One of the urban areas involved was my birthplace, the Los Angeles basin in Southern California. It once had one of the best trolley systems in the country. As a boy, I asked my father about the empty steel tracks in the street. He replied, "We used to have street-cars." Eventually the tracks were torn out or covered over. According to transit officials, these old facilities, which had carried millions of riders, could have provided the *affordable* core for public transit. Now, however, Southern California is badly polluted and congested, and, writes Kwitney, "in most American cities the rails and wires are gone."

In 1949, the responsible companies were convicted of criminal conspiracy in a federal court. Perhaps the judge was unaware of the tremendous significance of this particular crime, for he sentenced most of the guilty corporations to pay a $5,000 fine. Guilty individuals paid one dollar.

Though this example of criminal greed is not well known, and though it is not the sole cause of the shape of urban life in today's America, the dismantling of streetcar systems still has had a tremendous impact on our cities and lifestyle. Once public transportation provided a convenient, cheap, and ecologically sound way for city dwellers to get around. Today, unlike Europe, most American cities do not have viable public transportation. Thus we burn huge quantities of fuel and pollute the atmosphere.

The L.A. basin of my youth has changed. Today its freeways are virtual parking lots for creeping cars and trucks. Fumes poison the air while drivers fume about not getting anywhere. Smog and acid fog injure human health. Trees in the Coast Mountains die from air pollution. Much of L.A.'s land surface is covered with concrete or asphalt devoted to the car and truck. Greed in the realm of business has contributed to the impoverishment of life and the defiling of creation. The car has helped make much of Southern California ugly. I have seen orange groves, dairy farms, and strawberry fields become a land of freeways and smog.

This story is just one example of how disregard for limits of God's creation in *one area* can lead to harm and death in other areas. God is one, and his creation, too, is one interconnected whole, one interwoven fabric. The righteous, wise requirements of God's kingdom hold for nature and society alike. In fact, the Bible sees justice and righteousness in the social-moral realm as intimately connected with fertility and prosperity in the natural realm. The Bible does not separate these two realms, for both are God's creation and both are subject to his creative Word for all things (Pss. 33:4–9; 147:7–20).

Psalm 19 shows that God's law for creation and his law for humans belong together. On the one hand, in Psalm 72, justice and righteousness for the poor and needy lead to the fruitfulness of earth and society. On the other hand, wickedness (stealing, false witness, adultery, covetousness) leads to evil consequences in other spheres of life, including the natural realm. Violating God's orders in the realm of nature leads to moral evil. But we must say more. Violating God's limits for nature *is* moral evil. And in the long run (to speak to the heartbeat of America), it is bad business, foolish economics, and the destruction of wealth.

The commandments tell us to love our neighbor. According to Paul, God expects righteousness from Christians who walk by the Spirit (Rom. 6:4–13; 2 Cor. 5:21). He sums up righteousness as love for our neighbor, revealed in the Ten Commandments (Rom. 13:8–10). But one cannot love one's neighbor without taking care of creation. When we pollute, we can injure and literally kill our neighbor. If we use natural and other resources poorly, we steal from our neighbor, indeed from our own children and grandchildren, who may someday curse us. We destroy the earth and do "wrong to a neighbor" because we covet more than the Creator has allotted to us. This covetousness, says Paul in Colossians 3:5, is idolatry. Hence Paul's strong statement on greed: "the greedy . . . will [not] inherit the kingdom of God" (1 Cor. 6:10; cf. 5:11).

Covetousness is an attitude of worship that dethrones the Creator and elevates the creature in his place. In Romans 1:25, Paul declares, "They exchanged the truth about God for a lie and worshiped and served the creature rather than the Creator, who is blessed forever!" The irony is that when God and his norms for life are rejected, humans end up both worshiping and defiling the world they idolize.

Back to the enjoyment of wealth

Against this background of Creation and the Fall, we can understand two things that apply to material wealth. First, we are invited to enjoy the goodness of creation and to thank God for it. Second, the Creator's design and the Redeemer's purpose set limits to our enjoyment of his gifts. The biblical phrase "righteousness and justice" sums up both the right order for wealth and the limits by which alone the good remains good.

This two-fold perspective on material wealth is clearly set out in 1 Timothy 6:

> Godliness with contentment is great gain. . . . But if we have food and clothing, we will be content with that. People who want to get rich fall into temptation and a trap. . . . For the love of money is a root of all kinds of evil. . . . But you, man of God, flee from all this and pursue righteousness, godliness, faith, love. . . . Command those who are rich in this present world not to be arrogant nor to put their hope in wealth, which is so uncertain, but to put their hope in God, *who richly provides us with everything for our enjoyment.* Command them to do good, to be rich in good deeds, and to be generous and willing to share." (NIV)

Scripture never calls us to deny ourselves the enjoyment of creation, as if some things in the world—the body or wealth or art, perhaps—were bad in and of themselves. But the Creator forbids that anything of creation usurp his place in our hearts, and he does limit us to the goods that are *proper* to us: food, not poison; marriage, not free love; the truth, not false witness; and wealth, not injustice. Righteous love of our neighbor sets limits to our acquisition of wealth. And the ecological order of creation sets righteous limits to the technological wealth of nations.

The Cross

There is another reality that sets limits to our wealth, to our natural right to enjoy the goods of creation. That is the Cross of Jesus Christ. As Oliver O'Donovan writes in his profound book, *Resurrection and Moral Order:*

We are not invited now to live in the created order as though there had been no cross. The resurrection body of Christ bears nail-prints, and the life of those who follow him means taking up the cross. The path to full participation [in God's kingdom] lies through being excluded.

Discipleship, then, involves us in the suffering of exclusion from various forms of created good which are our right and privilege as Adam's restored children. (p. 95)

These words of O'Donovan echo our Lord, who said:

If any man would come after me, let him deny himself and take up his cross and follow me. For whoever would save his life will lose it; and whoever loses his life for my sake and the gospel's will save it. For what does it profit a man, to gain the whole world and forfeit his life? For what can a man give in return for his life? For whoever is ashamed of me and of my words in this adulterous and sinful generation, of him will the Son of man also be ashamed, when he comes in the glory of his Father with the holy angels. (Mark 8:34–38)

Many evangelicals in North America today appear to have forgotten these words of Jesus. But one cannot follow Christ to glory without first following him to Golgotha. The servant is not above his master. As Christ suffered self-denial and loss of the world for the sake of God's kingdom, so must his disciples. In a sinful, still broken world, Christians are called to suffer for the sake of the kingdom and its righteousness (2 Tim. 1:8; 2:3–11; 4:5). Second Timothy is quite clear on this point: "Indeed all who desire to live a godly life in Christ Jesus will be persecuted" (3:12). Christ himself is our model: "For you know the grace of our Lord Jesus Christ, that though he was rich, yet for your sake he became poor, so that by his poverty you might become rich" (2 Cor. 8:9).

The world with all its wealth belongs to Jesus Christ, its Maker, Lord, and Redeemer. And so it also belongs to those who are "in Christ," who were "bought with a price." "For all things are yours . . . [including] the world . . . [because] you are Christ's" (1 Cor. 3:21–22). Paul says of Abraham and his spiritual descendents that they will "inherit the world" (Rom. 4:13).

But the time of full inheritance is not yet. In this time before the end, sorrow and injustice, poverty and abuse still flourish. Therefore, Christians are called to suffer for Christ and his gospel of love. They are to die to self and the world. Christians use this present world, as they must, and even enjoy it in foretastes of the eternal Sabbath, but they do not treat it as ultimate (1 Cor. 7:29–31; 1 Tim. 6:17). Only God and his kingdom, a new heaven and a new earth in which righteousness dwells, is ultimate. For that kingdom we still wait (2 Pet. 3:13). Meanwhile, those who belong to Christ suffer as he did, doing works of righteous love.

This was Paul's ideal:

> Now I rejoice in my sufferings for your sake, and in my flesh I complete what is lacking in Christ's afflictions for the sake of his body, that is, the church. . . . (Col. 1:24)

> I count everything as loss because of the surpassing worth of knowing Christ Jesus my Lord. For his sake I have suffered the loss of all things, and count them as refuse, in order that I may gain Christ. . . . (Phil. 3:8)

The church that does not suffer is not the church of Christ. For we were baptized not only into his resurrection, but into his *death* (Rom. 6:1–23). This fundamental New Testament truth needs to be preached, heard, believed, and obeyed. It directly contradicts the popular preaching of those "depraved in mind and bereft of the truth, [who imagine] that godliness is a means of gain" (1 Tim. 6:5).

Proverbs and the false gospel of "health and wealth"

The Book of Proverbs is often mined for wisdom concerning wealth and poverty. But the message of this book is anything but a simplistic gospel of health and wealth. Proverbs requires Spirit-filled wisdom to understand and use its many-faceted sayings rightly: "Like a lame man's legs, which hang useless, is a proverb in the mouth of fools" (Prov. 26:7).

One group of biblical proverbs *does* point out a fundamental connection between godly righteousness and wealth, while another group highlights the connection between wickedness and poverty. Often the two contrasting thoughts appear in a single two-line verse:

"The LORD does not let the righteous go hungry, but he thwarts the craving of the wicked" (10:3). "In the house of the righteous there is much treasure, but trouble befalls the income of the wicked" (15:6). "Misfortune pursues sinners, but prosperity rewards the righteous" (13:21). Laziness is a type of wickedness: "He who tills his land will have plenty of bread, but he who follows worthless pursuits will have plenty of poverty" (28:19). Other, related proverbs simply seem to say that wealth is good and poverty bad: "A rich man's wealth is his strong city; the poverty of the poor is their ruin" (10:15, but see 18:10–11!). If we had only these proverbs and others like them, we might think that if you are godly, you must be rich. If you are poor, you must be bad. Job's "friends" thought he was bad because of his misfortune, but they were wrong.

We need to realize that proverbs, including biblical ones, are true *with regard to the particular situation that they fit.* This principle is not "situationalism"; it is just the nature of proverbs. What the German poet Goethe said of languages is better said of proverbs: "He who knows one, knows none." For example, of most marriages we might say, "Birds of a feather flock together." But there are some lovely couples of which we declare, "Opposites attract!" To one of our sons we usually say, "Look before you leap!" But his brother needs to be encouraged with "He who hesitates is lost!" Do Americans finally believe "Money talks" or "Money isn't everything"?

Proverbs 26:4 says, "Answer not a fool according to his folly. . . ." This advice is usually given in the Bible for dealing with fools (Compare the saying of Jesus, "Do not throw your pearls before swine."). But the next verse in Proverbs says, "Answer a fool according to his folly. . . ." The wise person will know which proverb fits his situation.

Another group of biblical proverbs shows that the good and godly can be poor, while the wicked prosper. It is not always true in this life that "the blessing of the LORD makes rich, and he adds no sorrow to it" (10:22). Proverbs knows that ". . . violent men get riches" (11:16b), that "the fallow ground of the poor yields much food, but it is swept away through injustice" (13:23), and that "there are those whose teeth are swords, whose teeth are knives, to devour the poor from off the earth, the needy from among men" (30:14).

In the context of a fallen world, wealth is not necessarily a sign of

God's blessing. It all hangs on whether wealth stays within the boundaries carved out by righteousness and justice, whether wealth serves the kingdom of God or the kingdom of the self. Proverbs is very plain on this point. "Better is a little with the fear of the LORD than great treasure and trouble with it" (15:16). "Better is a little with righteousness than great revenues with injustice" (16:8). "It is better to be of a lowly spirit with the poor than to divide the spoil with the proud" (16:19). "Better is a poor man who walks in his integrity than a rich man who is perverse in his ways" (28:6). In Scripture the choice between righteousness with poverty and wealth with injustice is clear. Jesus himself put our earthly needs and anxieties in the context of righteousness: "Seek first his kingdom and his righteousness, and all these things shall be yours as well" (Matt. 6:33).

The only prayer recorded in Proverbs is in harmony with this saying of Jesus:

> Two things I ask of thee;
>   deny them not to me before I die:
> Remove far from me falsehood and lying;
>   give me neither poverty nor riches;
> feed me with the food that is needful for me,
> lest I be full, and deny thee,
>   and say, "Who is the LORD?"
> or lest I be poor, and steal,
>   and profane the name of my God. (30:7–9)

These biblical perspectives on creational norms and limits to wealth are accentuated and deepened by the Fall. In our present world, the boundaries are massively eroded; God's limits are trampled on. And so troubles multiply, for we reap what we sow. Temporary prosperity is too often bought by violating the ecological limits of creation. "Toxic waste . . . hothouse effect . . . ozone depletion . . . smog . . . Chernobyl"—these are now household words. And in the social realm, the rich often build their kingdoms at the expense of God's kingdom, which includes the poor (Matt. 25:35–45; Lev. 25). People and nations spend and borrow beyond the limits of economic common sense.

But the Fall is not the last word. Our Redeemer came to save sinners and the creation, to restore them and it to righteousness—which includes economic affairs. Paul works out the practical implications of the Cross for financial stewardship. He writes to the Corinthians with inspired balance concerning his collection for the impoverished Christians in Jerusalem. The basis of Paul's appeal is this: "You know the grace of our Lord Jesus Christ, that though he was rich, yet for your sakes he became poor, so that you through his poverty might become rich" (2 Cor. 8:9, NIV). "The mind of Christ" should also be in us because we are his, bought with his blood and anointed with his Spirit.

God's kingdom has not fully come with goodness and justice for all. The bitter words of Ecclesiastes still echo in our minds:

> I saw under the sun that in the place of justice, even there was wickedness, and in the place of righteousness, even there was wickedness. . . . Again I saw all the oppressions that are practiced under the sun. And behold, the tears of the oppressed, and they had no one to comfort them. (Eccles. 3:16; 4:1)

It is in this sad context that we are called to follow Christ, to "invest in the kingdom of God," to be stewards of his good earth, until he comes again to wipe away every tear, to make *all things new*.

And yet, he invites us to enjoy his bounty even now (Eccles. 9:7–10; 1 Tim. 4:4–5; 6:17). In this world of woe, the enjoyment of creation remains an amazing grace of God, pure and simple. It testifies to our Maker's goodness and love. He invites us, in the earthly bread and wine, to taste and see that the Lord is good. He invites us in the bodily joy of marriage to recognize the mysterious love of Christ and his bride. For that wedding feast we still wait.

Come quickly, Lord Jesus.

Notes

1. See Hebrews 13:4, "let the marriage bed be undefiled." In Greek, "undefiled" is also used of the holy temple.

2. *Gerechtigkeit als Weltordnung.* See also his "Creation, Righteousness, and Salvation: 'Creation Theology' as the Broad Horizon of Biblical Theology," in B. W. Anderson, ed., *Creation in the Old*

Testament (Minneapolis: Augsburg Fortress, 1984), 102–17.

3. Greek *exousia* means both power and authority.

4. "Philippine Land Reform Stalls," *World Watch* 3/1 (January–February, 1990), 12.

5. Note well that in Leviticus, the release of land and slaves in jubilee followed only upon the "Day of Atonement," the great day of confession and forgiveness of sins. This pattern, which connects worship and social justice, is fundamental to the biblical world view. Scripture does not separate Sabbath from social justice, nor right worship from right practice. The prophets show that in the long run, neither is possible without the other.

6. In *Tending the Garden* (Grand Rapids: Eerdmans, 1987), edited by W. Granberg-Michaelson.

7. See G. Wenham's *The Book of Leviticus* (Grand Rapids: Eerdmans, 1979) on Leviticus 25; also Numbers 27:1–11; 36; 1 Kings 21.

8. See G. von Rad, *Wisdom in Israel* (Nashville: Abingdon, 1973), chapter 9.

Chapter 4

FALLOW TIME: AN EXPLORATION OF THE SABBATH AND WEALTH

David Neff

Wealth is stored-up work. In its various forms—savings accounts, insurance policies, bonds, cash, and commodities—it is an economic battery, charged up by yesterday's labor, and able to be converted to provide both tomorrow's needs and its delights.

By storing up the results of our labor, we are able to bridge the gulf of time: we set aside something "for a rainy day," we insure against catastrophic medical costs, we prepare for retirement or save for a college education.

Money gives us power over the future, or at least the illusion of power. For although money can be used to pay tuition, it cannot buy wisdom; although money can purchase medical insurance, it cannot buy health; although money can stake out a space for us in a sunny community on the Florida coast, it cannot buy us a long and happy life. All our attempts to bridge time and control the future can be foiled in the vulnerable moment when a vagrant blood clot hits the brain or a speeding vehicle hurtles across the expressway median to intersect our own trajectory.

God alone is Lord of time. He has given to us, his human creatures, dominion over space, over earth and sea, to be stewards of the species for their well-being and our own. But only Yahweh is the Lord of time, moving as he will through history, unhindered by the boundaries of sunsets and equinoxes. Our attempts to shackle time, to squeeze from the moments every drop of value, to control the clock by storing up labor, often become a tasting of forbidden fruit, a savoring of the vacant promise that we shall be as gods. And when we store up treasure on earth, God says to us, "Fool! This night your soul is required of you" (Luke 12:20).

A bridge across time

To spare his people that judgment, God gave them the Sabbath, a weekly rift in time across which is laid a bridge of grace. It was to be a time in which no work was done, and thus in which no future value was to be milked from it. All other time is a passage away from the past and a groping toward the future; but the Sabbath is pure present. The Sabbath is pure present moment because it is filled with the Shekinah, the Presence of God. As Abraham Joshua Heschel writes, "[W]hen the Sabbath is entering the world, man is touched by a moment of actual redemption; as if for a moment the spirit of the Messiah moved over the face of the earth."[1] And again, he speaks of the Sabbath as a time "when a beautifying surplus of soul visits our mortal bones and lingers on."[2] And as both pure present and pure Presence, the Sabbath deflects us from our hurtling course toward an uncertain future, and it assures us of love and grace in this moment.

The Lord of Time showed this day of Presence with a sign and with sustenance. Here is the tale of the giving of the Sabbath:

The Israelites, freed from oppression, from the exploitation of their labor by their Egyptian masters, had walked for six weeks through the desert toward the wilderness where Moses, their leader, had once tended sheep. They had felt the oppression of thirst, but at

Marah and Elim they had drunk the sweet, liberating waters. But now they felt the sting of hunger's lash and murmured their discontent.

The Lord chose the occasion to show them his Presence: "That I may prove them, whether they will walk in my law or not" (Exod. 16:4b). He fed them quail at twilight, and he feasted them at the dawn with bread—bread, fine as hoarfrost and white as coriander, and sweet, sweet as wafers made with honey.

Miraculously, this bread from heaven was given the same to all. No matter how much a person gathered, when it was measured out, it was the same as everyone else's—about half a gallon.

But divine benevolence is not without its limits. The Lord through Moses instructed them to clean their plates, to hoard not a mouthful of the supernatural food for another day. In the tents of those who did conserve, hedging against hunger by storing up the day's labor against the morrow's feared absence of miracle, sweetness turned bitter as the manna "bred worms and became foul" (Exod. 16:20). But there was indeed a miracle on the morrow, for the Lord of Time is never absent.

On the sixth day, the rhythm changed. When they measured out their gatherings, they had a full gallon for each person. "Tomorrow is a day of solemn rest," Moses relayed to the people, "a holy sabbath to the Lord" (Exod. 16:23). He bade them prepare what they would, by baking and boiling, and to lay it by till morning, for there would be no heaven-sent food on the ground on the Sabbath morn. Indeed, it came to pass: those who stored it as they were told found their food fresh; while those who went forth to gather in the seventh day's early light found nothing.

Thus is the Sabbath a day of both fullness and emptiness. To those who trust the Lord's sufficiency for the present, it is a day filled with sweetness. But to those who must relentlessly squeeze the teat of today to find milk for the morrow, it is emptiness. Those who go forth to gather find nothing to harvest.

"See! The Lord has given you the sabbath," said Moses. "Remain every man of you in his place . . . on the seventh day," he instructed. "So the people rested on the seventh day," he recorded (Exod. 16:29–30).

Just a few weeks later, the people trembled and the mountain quaked as Yahweh uttered ten words that initiated his covenant with Israel. In those words, he liberated them from the tyranny of inflamed desire. "You shall not covet your neighbor's house," he commanded. "You shall not covet your neighbor's wife, or his manservant, or his maidservant, or his ox, or his ass, or anything that is your neighbor's" (Exod. 20:17). These words warn against the fever that drives us to possess what must never be ours, whether that be the means of production (oxen and asses) or labor (manservants, maidservants), the fruits of someone else's work (thy neighbor's house), or his exclusive delights (thy neighbor's wife). And the word "You shall not steal" warns us away from clothing desire in action. It is a word to the dishonest and the bent among us.

But the Sabbath command is a word to the honest and hardworking, a warning to those who work happily to earn their rewards. The Sabbath warning is directed not to the slacker but to the one who takes responsibility—responsibility for family, for employees, for strangers, caring for them by providing rewarding and creative opportunities. It is addressed to those who, in their status as *imago Dei*, are compelled to bring order and to fight chaos. Fighting chaos means controlling tomorrow. Thus the temptation never to rest, never to let go and leave a minute fallow.

But it is precisely in his role as Subduer of Primordial Chaos that Yahweh identifies with his people and urges them to follow him not only into work, but also into rest. "Remember the sabbath day, to keep it holy . . . for in six days the Lord made heaven and earth, the sea, and all that is in them, and rested the seventh day; therefore the Lord blessed the sabbath day and hallowed it" (Exod. 20:8, 11).

Harvesting time and reaping fields

The Sabbath command is a parallel to the harvest laws of Leviticus 19: "When you reap the harvest of your land, you shall not reap your field to its very border, neither shall you gather the gleanings after your harvest. And you shall not strip your vineyard bare, neither shall you gather the fallen grapes of your vineyard; you shall leave them for the poor and for the sojourner: I am the Lord your God" (vv. 9–10).

The first command is about harvesting time; the second, about reaping fields. Both embody two principles: care for the future and care for the poor. Anxiety for the future is discouraged; but concern for the poor is cultivated.

Many who have been raised in strictly sabbatical homes were nurtured on the parable of the grasshopper and the ant. However, that parable was not spoken by our Lord, but inscribed in the gospel according to Aesop. And there is a great gulf fixed between the spirit of the slave fabulist and that of the Lord of Freedom, him who said:

> Do not be anxious about your life, what you shall eat or what you shall drink, nor about your body, what you shall put on. Is not life more than food, and the body more than clothing? ... If God so clothes the grass of the field, which today is alive and tomorrow is thrown into the oven, will he not much more clothe you, O men of little faith? Therefore do not be anxious, saying, 'What shall we eat?' or 'What shall we drink?' or 'What shall we wear?' For the Gentiles seek all these things; and your heavenly Father knows that you need them all. But seek first his kingdom and his righteousness, and all these things shall be yours as well. Therefore do not be anxious about tomorrow, for tomorrow will be anxious for itself. Let the day's own trouble be sufficient for the day. (Matt. 6:25, 30–34)

Of course, Scripture also contains the Book of Proverbs, which chastises the sluggard for his sloth and prophesies reward for the hard-working. The key is found in knowing the difference between, on the one hand, working hard enough and resting often enough to face the uncertainty of the future in confidence, and, on the other hand, facing the future with fear and, in desperation, working in self-defense, never resting in grace.

The land shall keep a Sabbath

The connection between the Sabbath and the harvest is carried further by the laws concerning the sabbatical year (Exod. 23:10–11; Lev. 25:1–7, 20–22; Deut. 15:1–11) and the year of jubilee (Lev. 25:8–17, 23–24).

Yahweh's command concerning a sabbatical year is that the land itself "shall keep a sabbath to the Lord." In an agrarian society, land is the fundamental form of wealth. On this foundation can be erected a modest estate or a fabulous fortune in cattle and corn. But without land, the agrarian is unable to amass wealth. Thus, if the people are to rest, the land too must keep a sabbath. Just as the human parties to the covenant are to work six days and keep sabbath on the seventh, the soil of the covenant land is to be cultivated and planted for six years, and in the seventh year to lie fallow. The crops that grow of themselves in that seventh year are not to be harvested, but to be gleaned by the poor and the wild beasts (Exod. 23:11) and to feed not only the landowners and their servants, but the sojourners, the cattle, and wild beasts (Lev. 25:6–7).

The sabbatical year was also the occasion for the forgiveness of debts, although such an amnesty applied only to fellow Hebrews (according to Deuteronomy 15:3, one could still exact payment from a foreigner).

For the creditor, debt is an asset, an account receivable. Like all forms of wealth, it can enslave its owner, for debt grants power to the creditor. It is not only money owed, but potentially people owned. Thus to be a creditor is to wield power, and to have power is to risk corruption.

For the debtor, debt is a binding to the past, a forced living with regret for actions long gone or with mourning for mishaps. As long as debt exists there is no rest, for tomorrow threatens to compound yesterday's sorrow. Thus if the covenant people—both debtors and creditors—are to experience rest and grace, debt must periodically be abolished.

The Lord understood the terrors that bind people to their assets, and he addressed those fears. Fear of not being repaid, because of an approaching sabbatical year, was not to discourage one from lending to a fellow Israelite in need: "Take heed lest there be a base thought in your heart, and you say, 'The seventh year, the year of release is near,' and your eye be hostile to your poor brother, and you give him nothing, and he cry to the Lord against you, and it be sin in you. You shall give to him freely, and your heart shall not be grudging when you give to him; because for this the Lord your God will bless you in all your work and in all that you undertake" (Deut. 15:9–10).

Likewise, fear of insufficient food was not to discourage one from letting the land lie fallow. Just as the sixth day's manna harvest lasted through the seventh day, the Israelites were promised that the sixth year's crop would be sufficient to tide them over the fallow year: "And if you say, 'What shall we eat in the seventh year, if we may not sow or gather in our crop?' I will command my blessing upon you in the sixth year, so that it will bring forth fruit for three years. When you sow in the eighth year, you will be eating old produce; until the ninth year, when its produce comes in, you shall eat the old" (Lev. 25:20–22).

In Matthew 6:25, Jesus surely echoed this promise, "Do not be anxious about your life, what you shall eat or what you shall drink, nor about your body, what you shall put on." In Matthew, Jesus' teaching about anxiety follows hard on his warning about the absurdity of trying to serve both God and Mammon (v. 24). And it initiates the paragraph that climaxes in his admonition to seek first the kingdom of God (v. 33). Both the sabbatical year and the Lord's teaching about anxiety are framed on the one side by freedom (from debt, from slavery), and on the other by responsibility to live out the covenant (the kingdom).

The sabbatical year is replete with gifts that, like Friday's excess manna, allow the Israelites to let time lie fallow. And as always, God ties the lack of taking care for the morrow to the necessity of caring for the poor. At the very time one is to show trust in God for the future, one is asked to stretch one's generosity in the present, to forgive freely and to lend without grudging. Thus generosity is piled onto generosity.

After seven sabbatical years was to come a year of jubilee. In the fiftieth year, not only was the land to lie fallow, but Israelites who had sold themselves into slavery because they were deep in debt were to be freed, and land was to be returned to the family of the original owner. The jubilee was a time of fresh starts and new beginnings. If the jubilee laws were observed, neither enormous wealth nor grinding poverty could be perpetuated through the generations. There could be no "culture of poverty" in which the collective memory of work and productivity had been erased.

In caring for the covenant people in this way, Yahweh said, "The land shall not be sold in perpetuity, for the land is mine" (Lev. 25:23a). Thus he refused to grant his people an absolute right to foundational wealth. The illusion of ownership easily evolves into the mirage of independence. But Yahweh did not wish his people to exercise independence; he wanted them to learn continued dependence on him. Thus he said, "The land shall not be sold in perpetuity, for the land is mine; for you are strangers and sojourners with me" (Lev. 25:23).

The sojourner's rootlessness cultivates dependency in the believer. The Sabbath, by suspending the daily routine, disorients the believer and encourages trust and dependence. The sabbatical year, by suspending the use of the land, disconnects the believer from terra firma, making him depend on God. The jubilee, by disrupting the relational world of property owners and indentured slaves, returns people to dependence on grace. The sojourner's experience of rootlessness is at the base of Israelite religion. In what is thought to be the earliest liturgical confession, the worshiper identifies himself thus: "A wandering Aramean was my father . . ." (Deut. 26:5).

Likewise, the experience of sojourn is a repeated theme in Mosaic ethics, from being a precursor of the Golden Rule, "You shall not oppress a stranger; you know the heart of a stranger, for you were strangers in the land of Egypt" (Exod. 23:9); to being a reason to keep the Sabbath, "You shall remember that you were a servant in the land of Egypt, and the Lord your God brought you out thence with a mighty hand and an outstretched arm; therefore the Lord your God commanded you to keep the Sabbath day" (Deut. 5:15).

Jesus and the jubilee

Just as Jesus' teaching on anxiety and trust echoed the sabbatical year, so his proclamation of his own ministry echoed the jubilee. In Luke's gospel, Jesus reads from the prophet Isaiah and then boldly claims that this message of liberation finds its fulfillment in him:

> The spirit of the Lord is upon me,
> because he has anointed me to preach good news to the poor.
> He has sent me to proclaim release to the captives
> and recovering of sight to the blind,
> to set at liberty those who are oppressed,
> to proclaim the acceptable year of the Lord.
> (Luke 4:18–19)

John Howard Yoder comments that whatever the phrase "the acceptable year of the Lord" may have meant to Isaiah, "for rabbinic Judaism, and thus for the listeners of Jesus it most likely meant ... the jubilee year, the time when the inequities accumulated through the years are to be crossed off and all God's people will begin again at the same point.... that there is to come into Palestine the equalizing impact of the sabbath year."[3]

Yoder goes on to cite André Trocmé's book *Jésus-Christ et la révolution non-violente* in which the author "has gathered the evidence that Jesus' concept of the coming kingdom was borrowed extensively from the prophetic understanding of the jubilee year."[4]

Scholars debate to what extent Israel ever experienced the full equalization of the jubilee. But at least once, during the time of Jeremiah, an Israelite king enforced the ancient law and declared all Hebrew slaves freed. Unfortunately, the slaveowners did nothing to help the slaves become economically self-sufficient, and they were soon back in bondage. Jeremiah protested this sad outcome and promised his countrymen punishment because they had failed to realize the jubilee's full liberation. Isaiah, writing of Israel's hope of restoration following the Babylonian captivity, used the jubilee language of economic readjustment to describe the fast that will draw Yahweh's attention:

> Is not this the fast that I choose:
>   to loose the bonds of wickedness,
>   to undo the thongs of the yoke,
> to let the oppressed go free,
>   and to break every yoke?
> Is it not to share your bread with the hungry,
>   and bring the homeless poor into your house;
> when you see the naked, to cover him,
>   and not to hide yourself from your own flesh?
> (Isa. 58:6–7)

In the same passage, the prophet urges the people to keep the Sabbath by avoiding their own business on God's holy day. But in the prophetic vision, harmony *(shalom)* is not restored to Israel simply by the observation of religious feasts or fasts. It is restored by the implementation of justice. Amos announces God's woe on those "who trample upon the needy," saying, "When will [the Sabbath] be over that we may sell grain ... and deal deceitfully with false balances, that we may buy the poor for silver and the needy for a pair of sandals?" (8:5–6). It is not alone the weekly cessation of commerce that sanctifies the seventh day. It is the extension of the Sabbath liberty from avarice throughout the week.

In the prophetic vision of a restored Israel, the principles and the practice of jubilee are realized. Each man sits under his own fig tree (Mic. 4:4); each plants his own vineyard and eats its fruit; each builds his own house and lives in it. No one is deprived of the fruit of his labor. No one is enslaved. All are brought to liberty (Isa. 61:1). And all observe the Sabbath together in the presence of the Lord (Isa. 66:23).

Jesus' vision of the kingdom of God likewise drew on Sabbath and jubilee imagery to present, in Yoder's words, "a visible sociopolitical, economic restructuring of relations among the people of God, achieved by his intervention in the person of Jesus as the one Anointed and endued with the Spirit."[5]

In Jesus' model prayer, a sequence of petitions explains his understanding of the plea "Thy kingdom come." First comes the petition for "daily bread," an obscure word in Greek, which may very likely be the equivalent of the Latin *diaria*, the daily food ration given out for the next day. Thus, according to a footnote in the Revised Standard Version, we pray, "Give us today our bread for the morrow." This petition grasps the assurance of pre-Sabbath manna and of the presabbatical year bumper crop. "Give us our bread for the morrow *in order that we may confidently enter into the jubilee.*"

Next comes release from debt. "Forgive us our debts as we forgive our debtors" recognizes the enslaving power of economic subordination. Debt in this prayer, says Yoder, is the "paradigmatic social evil."[6] This mutual entering into forgiveness of debt, of at once forgiving and being forgiven, is the only petition our Lord took the trouble to underscore with a warning. After finishing the prayer, he said, "For if you forgive men their trespasses, your heavenly Father also will forgive you; but if you do not forgive men their trespasses, neither will your Father forgive your trespasses" (Matt. 6:14–15).

That Jesus' vision of the kingdom involved economic restructuring along jubilee lines is clear from the number of parables he told relating to the forgiveness of debt and the alleviation of poverty and oppression:

The story of the unforgiving servant centers on the remission of debt and the proper response to forgiveness. The hardened servant was only too willing to plead for mercy and to accept gratefully forgiveness for his own enormous debt. But he was unmoved by the king's graciousness and threw into jail someone who could not pay him a debt only one twenty-thousandth of 1 percent of his own (Matt. 18:23–35).

The parable of the workers hired at different times, but all paid equally by the householder, employs an economic metaphor to stress God's desire to deal graciously and sovereignly with all of his creatures, and to see his grace experienced equally (Matt. 20:1–16).

The prodigal son wasted his inheritance and sold himself into servitude, but when he returned home asking to be a household servant in his father's house, the father restored him to the position of a son. How the money had been spent, or even that it had been spent, was not an issue for the father. The homecoming was a time for rejoicing (for that is what *jubilee* means), and therefore it was a time of debt remission and manumission (Luke 15:11–32).

The parable of Dives and poor Lazarus stresses the penalty the well-heeled will pay for ignoring gross economic suffering as well as the way God's justice in the afterlife will reward those who, in this life, have been victims of economic oppression (Luke 16:19–31).

The parable of the rich fool (Luke 12:13–21) displays the folly of the one "who lays up treasure for himself, and is not rich toward God." What does it mean to be rich toward God? The next pericope (Luke 12:22–34; cf. Matt. 6:25–34) urges trust in God and concludes with these familiar words: "Fear not, little flock, for it is your Father's good pleasure to give you the kingdom. Sell your possessions, and give alms; provide yourselves with purses that do not grow old, with a treasure in the heavens that does not fail, where no thief approaches and no moth destroys. For where your treasure is, there will your heart be also." Jesus' understanding of being "rich toward God" clearly involved more than an inner attitude of trust. It involved outer trusting activity that would enter into jubilee-like sharing.

The parable of the unrighteous steward is subject to various interpretations, but an important element in the story's structure is the forgiveness of debt (Luke 16:1–13).

Luke caps the telling of these parables by relating Jesus' encounter with a crooked tax collector (Luke 19:1–10). Zacchaeus' response to that encounter was "Behold, Lord, half of my goods I give to the poor; and if I have defrauded any one of anything, I restore it fourfold." Jesus' reply? "Today salvation has come to this house."

At least since Augustine's time, the church has promulgated a largely spiritual interpretation of these parables. And, in view of the oppressive sense of the kingdom delayed, such spiritualizing was to an extent necessary. But it seems clear from the gospel records that early in his ministry Jesus and his followers expected the kingdom to come within their lifetimes and that a jubilee-style economic reordering would not only be the result of the kingdom, it would be a mode of entrance into it. Indeed, when at Pentecost the Spirit fell upon the church, inaugurating the kingdom in this present age for those who would enter it, the automatic response of the believing community was one of economic leveling (Acts 2:43–47).

The possibility of a recovery

The spiritual meaning of wealth is the domination of time and exaltation of the self. The spiritual meaning of the Sabbath, the sabbatical year, and the jubilee is the dominion of Yahweh over time and the dependence of his people on his grace.

Wealth is an attempt to build a bridge across time, to store up the potential of labor to exercise control over the future. The Sabbath is a disciplined attempt to release control over time and to depend on grace.

Wealth is an attempt to gain independence from the community and from spiritual reality: He who has the gold makes the rules. But the jubilee and the sabbatical year teach that in reality interdependence and trust in God reflect the true character of existence.

The status of the Sabbath has been ambiguous in the church's history. Jesus' followers abandoned it, along with anything else that might have branded them as belonging to a sect of Judaism, within a hundred years after his death. The hellenization of the second-century church, and the incipient anti-Semitism that accompanied that process, discarded much that is rich in the church's Jewish heritage.

Yet at various times the church has rediscovered the Sabbath. Not finding New Testament warrant for treating Sunday as a sabbath, the continental Reformers rejected sabbatarianism as a papal innovation. For Calvin, as for Luther, there was an obligation to worship and an obligation to rest, but one day was as good as another under the New Covenant. The English Puritans, however, argued that the Sabbath was a creation ordinance, not just a Jewish ceremonial. And since the obligation of observing a particular holy day existed before Sinai, it also existed after the Cross. Unfortunately, in "rediscovering" the Sabbath, the Puritan divines failed to unfold its economic and social meaning as spelled out in the seventh and fiftieth years. For them it was almost pure command, and became as it were a third sacrament, a holy thing to be revered.[7]

Subsequent sabbatarianism in England and America, most notably under the influence of the Lord's Day Alliance and among Seventh-day Adventists, has continued this Puritan tradition that focuses on the holiness of a day and the ways to avoid transgressing it. Attention to the day's economic and social significance has surfaced only in recent years among Adventists and then only among that denomination's theologians. For the Adventist rank and file, the focus of Sabbath observance is on not transgressing the day's holiness.

The Sabbath's social and economic meaning may be largely lost to our atomistic society (although political changes such as Third World land reform may be undergirded by studying the jubilee). When only isolated pockets of believers incorporate the Sabbath discipline into their spirituality, it is nearly impossible to experience the Sabbath as freedom from economic bondage. It is possible, although difficult, for an individual to observe the holiness of a day. The support of a family and a congregation do much to reinforce that observance. But without a wide acceptance of the Sabbath's relevance for our time, the social and economic significance remain sealed off from experience. Nevertheless, the vision of the Sabbath, the seventh year, and the jubilee can do much to catechize us on our relation to wealth: Thou shalt remember the Sabbath, in order to exit anxiety and to enter into grace and trust, in order to leave behind the closed, grasping hand and to open the hand to generosity.

Notes

1. Abraham Joshua Heschel, *The Sabbath* (New York: Harper & Row, 1951, 1966), 68.

2. Ibid.

3. John Howard Yoder, *The Politics of Jesus* (Grand Rapids: Eerdmans, 1972), 36.

4. Ibid.

5. Ibid., 39.

6. Ibid., 41.

7. M. M. Knappen, *Tudor Puritanism: A Chapter in the History of Idealism* (Chicago: University of Chicago Press, 1939), 450.

Chapter 5

INVESTING IN WHAT LASTS

Wayne A. Grudem

All day long we are "investing" in using time, skill, energy, money, and possessions for various purposes—expecting some good return from the way we "invest" these things.

Some people make incredibly foolish choices and invest primarily in drugs, alcohol, or sex to gain immediate sensual pleasure. But they soon find these things to be cruel masters—they take all we invest and pay back destruction and early mortality, thus confirming that, even physically, "the wages of sin is death" (Rom. 6:23).

Others—including many Christians—invest their whole lives in things that seem benign or even praiseworthy: physical health, travel and recreation, even education. Yet these investments—as sound as they may be—pay no eternal rewards. Others invest years and dollars in acquiring power. Whether the goal is political, corporate, or ecclesiastical power, or power over public opinion through the media or education, these people seek the same things Jesus spoke of: "The rulers of the Gentiles lord it over them and their high officials exercise authority over them" (Matt. 20:25). Yet Jesus warns us, "It shall not be so among you" (Matt. 20:26).

Still others, like the rich fool, invest in gaining material wealth (honestly, or otherwise). But Jesus clearly taught that "a man's life does not consist in the abundance of his possessions" (Luke 12:15). Indeed, "We brought nothing into the world, and we cannot take anything out of the world" (1 Tim. 6:7).

So what is a worthy investment for a Christian's time, energy, and money?

Jesus calls us to invest all we have in a different goal: "Do not lay up for yourselves treasures on earth but lay up for yourselves treasures in heaven, where neither moth nor rust consumes and where thieves do not break in and steal. For where your treasure is, there will your heart be also" (Matt. 6:19–21). In a broad sense, even routine activities must be done with a view toward honoring God: "Whether you eat or drink, or whatever you do, do all to the glory of God" (1 Cor. 10:31).

Specifically, this means that all of our investment of time and skill, all of our use of money and possessions, must be used in ways that God approves. It is not just a question of giving a percentage of our income (or time) to the Lord: *All* that we have is a gift from him, and we are merely stewards of "our" skills and possessions. Paul rightly reminds the Corinthians, "What have you that you did not receive? If then you received it, why do you boast as if it were not a gift?" (1 Cor. 4:7). What skill do we have that we did not receive from God? What physical or intellectual ability? What friendship or family relationship, or job, or spiritual maturity, or moral ability? Indeed, every breath of air we draw is given from him (Acts 17:25).

Therefore, if God wished to demand 100 percent of our time and possessions, even with no reward paid us, we would have no just grounds on which to object. Yet God has done much more: He has promised us rewards—a "return" on our investments—both in this life and in the life to come if we invest our time and possessions in ways pleasing to him. This applies to our work, our use of possessions, and our expectations for heavenly rewards.

Investing time and strength

Even among Christians, few go to work on Monday morning thinking they are going to work for the Lord. But that is what Paul commands: "Whatever your task, work heartily, as serving the Lord and not men, knowing that from the Lord you will receive the inheritance as your reward; you are serving the Lord Christ" (Col. 3:24; cf. Eph. 6:6–7). Our daily work *is* pleasing to God, and it is rendering service to him—consistent with the fact that God gave work to Adam and Eve before there was any sin in the world: They were to "subdue" the earth and "have dominion" over everything on it (Gen. 1:28), and they were to "till" and "keep" the garden (Gen. 2:15). So work in itself is something "very good" in God's eyes (Gen. 1:31). Though there is pain in work because of the Fall (Gen. 3:17–19), work is still a blessing from God and something we can thank him for.

Should we work to become wealthy? If we do our work faithfully, God may or may not grant us wealth as a result. "In all toil there is profit" (Prov. 14:23), but in some toil there is more profit than in others. Nevertheless, our goal must never be to become wealthy: "Do not toil to acquire wealth; be wise enough to desist" (Prov. 23:4). We cannot serve both God and money (Matt. 6:24). Paul's warning against striving to become rich is strong and needs to be memorized by followers of a misleading "health and wealth gospel": "Those who desire to be rich fall into temptation, into a snare, into many senseless and hurtful desires that plunge men into ruin and destruction. For the love of money is the root of all evil; it is through this craving that some have wandered away from the faith and pierced their hearts with many pangs" (1 Tim. 6:9–10).

We sometimes value jobs as the world does: more status and more pay signify more importance. But our goal in our work should not be acquiring wealth or status, but rather being faithful to God whether our tasks be (in the world's sight) large or small. This lesson is in the parable of the talents (Matt. 25:14–30): Each servant who was faithful with what he had been given received his master's commendation, "Well done . . . you have been faithful over a little, I will set you over much" (Matt. 25:21, 23). That commendation is what we, too, should seek—after all, what is earthly wealth or fame compared to the "Well done" of the Lord of heaven and earth?

This should give us satisfaction no matter what kind of work we do. We do it for him! "Whatever good anyone does, he will receive the same again from the Lord, whether slave or free" (Eph. 6:8). Often our work will involve earning a living (1 Thess. 4:11–12; 2 Thess. 3:6–12). For many Christians it will involve caring for children and households (Prov. 31:27–31; 1 Tim. 5:10, 14). At other times it will involve work to help the church (1 Pet. 4:10). These jobs are to be done trusting God for the appropriate reward.

And there *will be* reward for doing our work as to the Lord, reward far greater than earthly wealth. Paul reminds managers to treat those under their authority "justly and fairly, knowing that you have a Master in heaven" (Col. 4:1), thus suggesting God expects fair and thoughtful management practice. On the other hand, those who work hard and are not rewarded adequately in this life are called to trust that God will be true to his Word, and will ultimately reward "whatever good anyone does" (Eph. 6:8). Scripture says, "From the Lord you will receive the inheritance as your reward; you are serving the Lord Christ" (Col. 3:24). Even if we "do right and suffer for it," and "take it patiently," we "have God's approval" (1 Pet. 2:20), and he will not forget.

Investing money and possessions

Not only our time and effort, but also the money and goods that God has given us must be "invested" in ways that will bring God's approval and fulfill his purposes.

Does this mean we have to give all that we have to the church, or to the poor? Though Jesus asked that of the rich young ruler (Matt. 19:21), he did not ask it of others who came to him, but rather he spoke to each person in terms of the particular area of resistance to his lordship that person needed most to hear (cf. John 4:16). Rather than giving away all that we have, we are required by Scripture to develop and use our resources as "faithful stewards," just as those who were faithful in the parable of the talents and the parable of the pounds (Luke 19:11–27; cf. 1 Cor. 4:1–2; 1 Pet. 4:10). We must do both: use some resources in ways pleasing to God, and give away some resources in ways that please him. Both using and giving away are investments in the work of God.

What uses of possessions are pleasing to God? First, God is glorified when we simply *enjoy*—with thanksgiving to him—the abundant resources of his good earth (Gen. 1:26, 28; Acts 2:46; 14:16–17). To command people to abstain from "foods which God created to be received with thanksgiving" is to give in to "deceitful spirits and doctrines of demons" (1 Tim. 4:1, 3). In fact, Paul says that God "richly furnishes us with everything to enjoy" (1 Tim. 6:17). Thus, we can glorify God by using the products of the earth with joy and thanksgiving.

Similarly, it is right to use some of our resources to increase the productivity of the earth—whether through planting more crops, developing more effective computers, or building more efficient factories. This is fulfilling God's purpose for us to "subdue" the earth and "have dominion" over it, thus making it useful and productive for our benefit as well as his glory. An unbeliever may produce material goods simply to increase his or her own wealth and power, but a Christian can build the same kind of factory or invest in the same kind of computer company with a desire to please God and be a faithful steward. One investor is serving money; the other, God.

But while investing in such material productivity is good, the emphasis of the New Testament is clearly on investing in something better: "spiritual productivity." We invest in spiritual productivity when we give generously to the work of the church (1 Tim. 5:17–18; Gal. 6:6; 1 Cor. 9:3–14; Phil. 4:15–18). This is directly helping the work of God's kingdom, because it is building on the foundation of the church with "gold, silver, precious stones," which will be tested with fire on the day the Lord returns (1 Cor. 3:12–13). This testing will disclose whether our giving has been for the Lord's glory rather than our own, and has been done in methods consistent with scriptural teachings.

One of the most common New Testament ways of investing for spiritual productivity is giving to the needs of others. Though such giving involves physical, material goods, it has rich spiritual implications: We show Christ's love through such gifts, for he says, "By this will all men know that you are my disciples, if you have love for one another" (John 13:35). And we evidence lack of Christ's love within us when we fail to meet the needs of other Christians (1 John 3:17). In giving food and drink to one of the least of Christ's brothers, we are ministering to Christ himself (Matt. 25:40).

Paul clearly demonstrated this concern by devoting the second half of his third missionary journey to taking up a collection for the needy Christians in Jerusalem (Rom. 15:25–27; 2 Cor. 8–9). In fact, he seemed to think that gentile Christians in Greece, though separated from the Jerusalem Christians by culture and distance, had an *obligation* to help fellow Christians in need: "They *ought* to be of service to them in material blessings" (Rom. 15:27, italics added). Here Paul specifies no 10 percent limit, but emphasizes generous giving, "for God loves a cheerful giver" (2 Cor. 9:6), and "he who sows bountifully will also reap bountifully" (2 Cor. 9:5). We are to give until the need is met (2 Cor. 8:15; cf. 1 John 3:17; Matt. 25:36–40). In all this we imitate—and thereby glorify—our Lord Jesus Christ, who, "though he was rich, yet for your sake he became poor" (2 Cor. 8:9).

Though the New Testament emphasis is on giving to the needs of other Christians, it is not exclusively so: "As we have opportunity, let us do good to all men, and especially those who are of the household of faith" (Gal. 6:10). When we give to help unbelievers, even our enemies, we glorify God because we reflect his own character of mercy and love: "But love your enemies, and do good, and lend, expecting nothing in return; and your reward will be great, and you will be sons of the Most High; for he is kind to the ungrateful and the selfish. Be merciful, even as your Father is merciful" (Luke 6:35–36).

Scripture tells us that those who are "rich in this world"—and that includes most Christians in modern industrialized societies—have a special obligation to invest in heavenly reward by giving to the needs of others. When Paul gives specific instructions for Christians who are "the rich in this world" (1 Tim. 6:17–19), he does not say that it is wrong for them to be rich, but he does say they are to be especially generous in their giving. They are "to do good, to be rich in good deeds, liberal and generous, thus laying up for themselves a good foundation for the future, so that they may take hold of the life which is life indeed."

Trusting God for rewards

Scripture motivates believers to give by referring to the rewards of generosity: We can trust God to provide us "enough" in this life, and "abundance" in heaven if we obey him. But the notion of reward carries with it a spiritual perspective. Paul reminds the Philippians, who have sent a generous gift to him, "My God will supply every need of yours according to his riches in glory in Christ Jesus" (Phil. 4:19). He reminds the Corinthians, as he encourages generous giving, that "God is able to provide you with every blessing in abundance, so that you may always have enough of everything and may provide in abundance for every good work" (2 Cor. 9:8; cf. Matt. 6:28–30; 1 Tim. 6:6–8; Heb. 13:5).

Often such provision comes in the fellowship of the church: Jesus, knowing of the sharing of relationships and possessions that will occur in the church, promises that whatever has been relinquished for his sake will be abundantly replaced: "There is no one who has left house or brothers or sisters or mother or father or children or lands, for my sake and for the gospel, who will not receive a hundredfold now in this time, houses and brothers and sisters and mothers and children and lands, with persecutions, and in the age to come eternal life" (Mark 10:29–30). In this age, we can trust God, not to make us wealthy (the New Covenant never promises that), but to supply all our needs.

But what will happen in the age to come? Here I think it will surprise almost all modern Christians (at least in the United States) to find how often the New Testament motivation for giving is promise of greater heavenly reward. This is why Jesus reminds us not to lay up treasures on earth, but tells us, "Lay up for yourselves treasures in heaven." The reason? "For where your treasure is, there will your heart be also" (Matt. 6:19–20). When those who are rich in this world are generous in their giving, they are thereby "laying up for themselves [literally, 'treasuring up for themselves'] a good foundation for the future, so that they may take hold of the life which is life indeed" (1 Tim. 6:18–19).

In fact, the New Testament will amaze us if we begin to count the number of times it emphasizes making sacrifices for the Lord's work here in order to seek a greater heavenly reward. In many passages, the idea of "investment" in God's work is closely connected to the clear teaching that God will ultimately and abundantly repay that investment: "Love your enemies, and do good, and lend, expecting nothing in return; and your reward will be great" (Luke 6:35). We are to invite those who cannot repay us for dinner—"the poor, the maimed, the lame, the blind"—and Jesus tells us "you will be blessed, because they cannot repay you. You will be repaid at the resurrection of the just" (Luke 14:13–14). And in our daily work, we know "that whatever good anyone does, he will receive the same again from the Lord, whether he is a slave or free" (Eph. 6:8). Paul mentioned reward in explaining how he delighted to preach the gospel without charge (1 Cor. 9:17–18), and many other verses have similar themes (Matt. 19:21; Luke 6:22–23; 1 Cor. 3:8; 2 Cor. 5:10; Gal. 6:9–10; Eph. 6:7–8; Heb. 10:34–35; 1 Pet. 1:4; 2 John 8; Rev. 11:18).

So the New Testament does not teach us simply to give away possessions for the sake of giving them away or appearing virtuous. Nor does it encourage us to adopt a "simple lifestyle" because simplicity has merit in itself. Rather, all of these commands are put in the context of glorifying God and furthering the work of his kingdom, and of laying up treasure in heaven and increasing our heavenly reward.

So the question is not "Shall we adopt a simple lifestyle?" nor is the question "Will God make us wealthy?" For those questions are too exclusively focused on this world.

An overemphasis on a simple lifestyle can burden us with false guilt and lead us to be poor stewards. Unnecessary self-denial may actually hide our talents (Matt. 25:25). We spend so much time caring for basic necessities of life that we become less productive in the work God has called us to do and are therefore far less able to give to the needs of others.

On the other hand, an overemphasis on becoming wealthy will lead us to the twin sins of selfishness and wastefulness, and we will disregard the needs of others and the church, hinder the work of the kingdom, and greatly diminish our heavenly reward. In addition, both the simple lifestyle and the wealth emphases neglect the spiritual, heavenly dimension that is so crucial to the Bible's teachings on our possessions.

The more important question we must ask ourselves is this: In all our use of time and wealth, are we really investing in ways that we know are pleasing to God so that we are continually, in all our actions, laying up treasures in heaven?

Perhaps the solution to our excessive materialism is worship. Perhaps we need to have our investment strategy changed through experiencing what greater joy there is in fellowship with the Lord and in service for him.

"O taste and see that the Lord is good! Happy is the man who takes refuge in him!" (Ps. 34:8).

Chapter 6

CALLED TO
SHARE

Pedrito U. Maynard-Reid

Traditional (or shall we say popular) stewardship theology in many contemporary churches runs something like this: Pay a tithe of your earnings to take care of the ministry and give a generous offering to take care of the other basic necessities of the church. Thus, biblical stewardship for some Christians is a relationship with the financial structure of the church. For those of us who grow up in a free-market economic system where individualism is an ideal, what we do with the rest of our wealth has nothing to do with Christian stewardship.

The New Testament, however, teaches a holistic view where stewardship involves all one has and does. This wider view of stewardship leads many to think the New Testament teaches us not to be wealthy, but it does not do that. Nowhere do we find a call for the church to be poor and to divest itself of wealth. There is, however, an overriding concern regarding the wealthy. They are presented in a negative light, in part because of their stewardship. That is, what they do with their wealth, not wealth *per se*, is condemned. Of course, wealthy people are strongly chastised for their flagrant oppression and injustice, but in many instances they are simply failing to participate in the desacralization of wealth by sharing it. Wealth is not necessarily bad, but a failure to share it with those in need is always wrong.

This biblical teaching is clear in the most precise New Testament passage dealing with Christian stewardship. Paul, writing to the Corinthian church, makes a radical call for equality. He pastorally pleads, "I do not mean that others should be eased and you burdened, but that as a matter of equality your abundance at the present time should supply their want, so that their abundance may supply your want, that there may be equality" (2 Cor. 8:14–15).

This classic passage on stewardship is a surprising text for an urban, Western, Greek church. We usually associate such language with the rural Palestinian or poor urban Jerusalem church. But this radical call for equality was not based on time and space. It was part of the transformed relationship God expected of all his people.

The earliest church realized that what the believers possessed came by the grace of God and must therefore be used in accordance with his character—character grounded in sharing. Thus, Paul could write to the Philippian church, "Let each of you look not only to his own interests, but also to the interests of others" (Phil. 2:4). He then followed this with the example of Jesus Christ, who did not count equality with God a thing to be grasped, but shared himself with humanity, even to the point of death on the cross (vv. 5–8).

The theme of sharing one's wealth as part of one's stewardship flows through the entire New Testament, but it is more dominant in the Synoptics-Acts and James due to their Palestine provenance. It is mostly in these writings that we learn what happens when this type of holistic stewardship is either neglected or followed.

The wages of selfishness
There are two clear negative outcomes for anyone who fails to participate in this lifestyle: condemnation and failure to share in the

final eternal rewards of the Christian believer.

Two parables illustrate the condemnation in store for those who do not share from their bounty: the rich man and Lazarus (Luke 16:19–31), and the rich fool (Luke 12:16–21). In both of these parables Jesus is not reported as being concerned with how the wealthy men obtain their riches. He is not concerned in these parables as to whether they exploited their workers or even Lazarus at the gate. The overriding concern of Jesus was what they did with their wealth and surplus possessions. The rich man in Luke 16 had no concern for Lazarus. The rich fool thought only of himself. They are condemned for not sharing their abundance with those who lack the basic necessities and for thinking only of themselves.

But there is also another subtle area for condemnation. Besides not sharing, there seems to be an implicit condemnation of the luxurious living of the wealthy. It is possible that the detailed description of the rich man in the story with Lazarus (he was "clothed in purple and fine linen and . . . feasted sumptuously every day" [Luke 16:19]) was intended to denounce such a lifestyle.

This seems to be most definitely the case in the Epistle of James where in 2:3 the man with "gold rings and fine clothing" is viewed negatively (v. 6) and in 5:2–3 where all these luxury items are cast upon the dust heap of eternity. In contrast to such, Jesus draws attention to John the Baptist's life of simplicity, contrasting it with the lifestyle of the wealthy, and thus implicitly commends his simplicity (see Luke 7:25).

The biblical data, therefore, seem to recognize that "fine clothing," "gold rings," and "sumptuous meals"—all symbols of luxury—might hamper the call to Christian social equalization. That is, such symbols have the power to separate people who otherwise might enjoy Christian fellowship.

Beyond the condemnation for failing to practice this radical stewardship is the loss of one's final reward. Indeed, those who hoard their possessions will receive eternal punishment. Again the story of the rich fool illustrates this point. He was attempting to "lay up treasures for himself" (Luke 12:21) in this life, but he lost out on the eternal treasures.

Even more forceful is the story of the rich ruler who desired to inherit eternal life. Jesus said, "One thing you still lack. Sell all that you have and distribute to the poor and you will have treasure in heaven." After he became sad, Jesus looked at him and said, "How hard it is for those who have riches to enter the kingdom of God! For it is easier for a camel to go through the eye of a needle than for a rich man to enter the kingdom of God" (Luke 18:22, 24–25).

We need to read this narrative literally and as rigorously as Jesus intended his words to be understood. It is a pity that Christian interpreters a century or so later—not coming to grips with the stringency of the saying, and anxious to conciliate the wealthy who were joining the church—invented the meaning of "rope" for the Greek word "camel" or also suggested that the "eye of the needle" was a small gate in Jerusalem through which a camel could pass only on its knees!

For Jesus, however, if the wealthy of his day intended to have treasures in heaven and eternal life, they had to give up the wealth that they had gained selfishly and oppressively, and share their wealth with the less fortunate. This is not an isolated teaching. In Luke 12:32–34, Jesus demands selling of one's possessions and giving alms as a prerequisite for heavenly treasures.

But even more sad than the loss of such treasure is the final destruction that will befall the wealthy who fail to share with the poor. It is interesting to note that according to the prophet Ezekiel, the reason God destroyed Sodom was because of its refusal to share with the poor (16:49–50).

And as it was in the case of Sodom, so it will be for Christians who fail to participate in this call to be stewards. This is the basic point of James's diatribe against the rich and his prophecy of their ultimate destruction (James 1:9–11; 5:1–6).

Again, it is a pity that interpreters of James from the second century until today have tried to evade the rigor of his teaching. They have attempted to spiritualize the passages by making "poor" equal to "poor in spirit," and "rich" equal to "non-Christian." They have tried to eliminate the social economic force of the text, and in so doing they have downplayed the judgment on the oppressive rich to whom James is addressing his malediction. Those who refuse to allow the poor to participate in their wealth will ultimately "fade away" (James 1:11). It is the natural result of those who spurn the call to share.

The rewards of sharing

For those who are willing to participate in the lifestyle of holistic stewardship, however, there are clear positive outcomes. Those who willingly share are singled out and commended for their generosity. For example, Paul praised the Macedonian believers because "they gave according to their means . . . and beyond their means, of their own free will" (2 Cor. 8:3).

But it is important to note that the believers did not demonstrate their stewardship to obtain praise. Instead, they realized that sharing and caring for the needy and marginal was "pure and undefiled religion" (James 1:27). It was a demonstration of God's love abiding in them (John 3:17). It was a proof of discipleship.

This point of discipleship should not be quickly passed over. A key criterion for becoming a disciple is sharing. Before the rich ruler could come and follow Jesus he had to "sell . . . and distribute to the poor" (Luke 18:22). Without doing that, he could not be part of a group that was a sharing community. Jesus and his disciples shared a common purse (John 12:6). The women traveling with Jesus shared their financial resources with Jesus and his disciples (Luke 8:1–3; Mark 15:40–41). There was oneness in sharing, without which they could not be Christ's disciples.

An automatic result of this oneness is that it would convince the world to believe in Jesus (John 17:20–23). The evangelistic impact of this radical stewardship in the early church is very clear in the Book of Acts where we find the repeated phrases, "and the Lord added to their numbers day by day those who were being saved" (2:47); "and with great power the apostles gave their testimony" (4:33); "and the word of God increased" (6:7).

All these reports of the evangelistic success of the church appear in the context of the sharing practiced by the early church. It was not a failed experiment, as some have suggested, but a vital part of their discipleship, which had a profound impact upon non-Christians. It was part of what Ronald Sider calls (in *Rich Christians in an Age of Hunger*) a "redeemed economic relationship where there was unlimited economic liability for, and total economic availability to, the other members of Christ's body."

The greatest result of such a Christian lifestyle is the ultimate reward of salvation. Zacchaeus's redeemed lifestyle elicited the words from Jesus, "Today salvation has come to this house" (Luke 19:9). He was no longer among the rich upon whom Christ had pronounced his woes (see Luke 6:24). He was now a disciple of Christ to whom salvation had come.

It is in this context that we must understand the dialogue with Jesus when he was asked, "Then who can be saved?" (Luke 18:26). For Jesus, whoever was willing to give up all for the kingdom—whoever was willing to be generous toward those who suffer for lack of the basic necessities—these will receive abundantly more in this time, and in the age to come, eternal life (Luke 18:29–30).

The pattern of the New Testament church, then, was one in which those who had abundance would supply the want of those who lack "that there may be equality" (2 Cor. 8:14). It was a pattern in which the haves and the have-nots experienced social and spiritual equality. It was part of their call to be Christian stewards.

Chapter 7

THE BENEVOLENT TRADITION OF WOMEN

Karen Halvorsen

Jesus' portrait of the charitable woman in Mark 12:41–44 is the emblem of a continuous tradition within the church: a feminine tradition of benevolence born in spite of cultural restrictions. Consider his description of this poor widow who donated two copper coins to the treasury: "... she gave everything she had, her whole being." In another time, this woman might have lived in a castle or a cloister, a settlement or a city, but, although less likely to receive from her contemporaries the recognition Jesus gave her, her philanthropic spirit would continue to express itself through acts of financial service.

Like the scribes, Christ often had his financial needs met by women. But, unlike the scribes, he did not "devour widows' houses" (Luke 20:47). The group of Galilean women who accompanied Jesus in his travels and ministered to him and his disciples "out of their means," as Luke 8:2–3 says, included Mary Magdalene, Joanna, Susanna, and "many others." They were treated as companions, an anomaly in a culture that transferred a woman from the guardianship of her father to that of her husband. These arrangements included financial control as well; a woman rarely took responsibility for her own funds until after her husband's death, or until her husband decided to divorce her.

It is unclear how these women freed themselves from the familial and financial strictures of ancient Palestine; it is clear that Jesus gratefully accepted their support. The reciprocity of these relationships is clearly seen in the interaction between Christ and Mary of Bethany. Because of her love and gifts of hospitality, Jesus allowed Mary to sit at his feet and learn from his lessons. In response, she took an "alabaster flask of pure nard, very costly," and anointed him. The oil was worth about three hundred denarii—often a whole year's wages for a vineyard worker. Her sense of the greater purpose of Christ's mission inspired her to make this costly sacrifice.

Within the limitations of his Roman culture, Paul would follow Christ's example of acceptance and validation of female support. During the early missionary period, gender did not define leadership roles as did the capacity to serve. Newly baptized Christians asserted that all were united in Jesus Christ—there were no distinctions between Jew and Gentile, free and slave, male and female; all were children of God. This egalitarian vision affirmed women as active and equal members of the community.

At this point in history, the most weighty factor in determining a woman's role in the church was clearly her social status. From New Testament times until recently, wealthy, well-connected women have had more opportunity to assert leadership and authority amid congregations.

The wealthy members of the nascent church offered their homes as sanctuaries. These house churches played an important role in early Christianity. Here Christians were free to celebrate the Eucharist and preach the gospel. Paul cites several women who founded churches within their homes, including Chloe of Corinth, Nympha of Colossae, and Priscilla, who was in business with her husband, Aquila. Priscilla and Aquila were tentmakers and supported their missionary efforts through their work. Together, they established and led house churches in Corinth, Ephesus, and Rome.

Like these hostesses, Lydia used her wealth as a bridge between the economic and ecclesiastical realms. Lydia is described as a "dealer in purple" (Acts 16:14). Though a Gentile, she attended Jewish services and supported the synagogues. Her desire for spirituality would lead her to become the first convert from Paul's preaching in Europe. Her financial income allowed her to establish and support a church for the people of Thyatira, as well as to provide a refuge for Paul.

Two of the five offices established in the Book of Acts and the Pauline epistles were designated for women: widows and deaconesses. In Romans 16:1–2, Paul mentions Phoebe, a prominent person who filled such an office. Her title is *"diakonos"* of the church at Cenchrea—a term translated as minister, missionary, or servant when in reference to men, and as deaconess in conjunction with Phoebe. Paul also calls Phoebe *prostatis*—"a helper of many and of myself [Paul] as well" (Rom. 16:2). Technically, this term referred to a patron or legal representative, or strangers who were deprived of civil rights. Apparently Phoebe carried authority in the community, perhaps offering financial aid and legal assistance, as well as hospitality and wisdom.

As the church developed, male leadership became dominant and made the role of women marginal. Widows and deaconesses, however, were allowed to maintain their offices throughout the early centuries of the church, or they performed charitable services with the help of money inherited or earned. Olympias (368–408), a deaconess in the church at Constantinople, used her inheritance to buy the freedom of hundreds of slaves, gave to the poor, relieved suffering, and built a monastery. She, along with many other women of her time, chose the humility of poverty over the comforts of wealth.

The poverty of Olympias was a manifestation of the great ascetic movement, which offered well-born Roman women the opportunity to serve the church in dramatically untraditional roles. By giving their material wealth as well as their whole selves to the church, they could live independently in study and spiritual development. The sacrifices of worldly pleasures, sex, and childbearing were the same as those made by men of that time, and they opened up the doorways to radical service.

Marcella (325–460) adopted this ascetic life. Known throughout Rome for her wealth and beauty, she chose to pursue her love for the Scriptures. After her husband died, she followed the examples of monks living in the desert and turned her Roman palace into a retreat for women. The church father Jerome would visit her there, at one point remaining for three years, studying and discussing the Scriptures with his hostess and her companions. Marcella's retreat, however, became more than a house of study; she soon opened one of the first hospitals in Rome and spent much of her immense fortune caring for the sick and dying. When the problems of the city became too great, she established the first convent for women, choosing the outskirts of Rome to construct a complete sanctuary.

Jerome writes of Marcella's death: Plunderers sacked the city, looted wealthy houses, and discovered Marcella; she received them without alarm, and when they looked for her gold, she pointed to her coarse, brown dress to prove that she had chosen poverty; they whipped her, but Marcella is said to have felt no pain at this treatment; rather, she threw herself at their feet to beg that her life might be taken instead of the life of a younger friend.

Jerome found further inspiration and support from another aristocratic Roman widow, Paula (347–404). After her conversion—which was brought about by Marcella—Paula also chose an ascetic life, giving to the poor and protesting against materialism. She exchanged her opulent litter for an ass, her fine foods for bread and oil, and her bed for a pallet of goat's hair. She built monasteries, churches, and hospitals. She then accompanied Jerome to Jerusalem, where they used her money to establish three nunneries and a monastery that served as sanctuaries for the needy. She aided Jerome in his work of translation, and she bought rare books and manuscripts essential to his task. He would dedicate his version of Job, Isaiah, Samuel, Kings, Esther, Galatians, Philemon, Titus, and the twelve minor prophets to Paula and her daughter Eustochium. He wrote: "What bedridden man was not supported with money from her purse?"

As the Medieval period approached, church offices dedicated to women were phased out. At the Synod of Orleans in 533, the office of deaconess was officially nullified "... on account of the weakness of the sex." Women found alternatives for service within monastic communities, ministering to each other and to the needy. Because nunneries demanded that postulants provide dowries, entrance into these communities was contingent on wealth. Increasingly, wealthy families paid for the construction of monasteries as a sign of prestige. Yet, in spite of this elitism and these less-than-spiritual motivations, the growing number of convents offered women opportunities for self-development and financial administration. A woman might even invest in the establishment of a monastery, secure the position of abbess through her monastery donations, and hold authority over nuns *and* monks.

Clare of Assisi (1194–1253) was cofounder with Francis of Assisi of the Franciscan Order of Poor Clares. She was born into a noble family and spent her girlhood in an atmosphere of wealth and culture. When her father died, Clare had already established her order, and she gave all her considerable inheritance to hospitals and the poor. During her lifetime, Clare founded branches of the Poor Clares in Italy, France, and Germany. She would maintain her vow of absolute poverty and service. During her last illness, Pope Innocent IV visited her twice and heard her confession. As he absolved her, he is reported to have said, "Would to God I had so little need of absolution."

Elizabeth of Hungary (1207–31) was the daughter of a king and the wife of a prince, but, inspired by stories of Clare, she surrendered her riches for a Franciscan robe and took on the role of a servant. Working with her husband, Elizabeth opened shelters for lepers, started soup kitchens, and built refuges for the homeless. When her husband died of a fever, Elizabeth took the vows of the Third Order of Saint Francis and continued her service to lepers, the aged, and the poor. She died spinning wool into cloth for the needy—at the age of twenty-four—apparently from exhaustion. Four years later, she was declared a saint, and two hundred thousand people gathered near her grave to do her honor.

From convent to kitchen
With the Reformation, public ministry—typified by the convent— was condemned by the Protestant church while the domestic world

was established as the realm for women. Financial service was most often a gesture of hospitality. Women opened their homes and cupboards to Protestant travelers and refugees.

The Reformed church in France had staunch and powerful supporters in Margaret (1492–1549) and her daughter, Jeanne (1528–72), the queens of Navarre, a kingdom in southern France. Although Margaret never publicly became a Protestant, she opened her palace to the Reformers. There, they preached and offered Communion in safety. Margaret's daughter, Jeanne, inherited her mother's passion for the Reformation. She carried on the tradition of holding services in her palace apartments. She established a large grant for a college of theology and financed household chaplains in their translation of the New Testament into the Basque dialect. She saw the great need of the Basque people, who had been Christians since the fifth century, but had no Bible in their own language.

Other patronesses of this time included Lady Armyne (1594–1675), who gave liberally for the conversions of Indians in New England; Isabella Bresegna (1510–67), who used her wealth to oppose papal authority during the Inquisition; and Anne Pembroke (1599–1674), who poured her money into charitable concerns, particularly care for the poor and sick. Selina, Countess of Huntingdon in England, is of special interest. After she was converted in 1739, she used her wealth to erect chapels throughout England and a college for preachers at Trevecca.

During the colonization and denominationalism of the seventeenth and eighteenth centuries, women found outlets for organized charity within dissenting religious movements. If, however, they were unable or unwilling to rebel against the standard of church authority, they rarely moved outside their roles as mothers and wives. Puritan society allowed women limited control of financial affairs, but as years passed and congregations became crowded with women, and as many men withdrew from church communities, the contributions of women became harder to ignore despite restraining forces. In acknowledging that women were "the hidden ones," Cotton Mather challenged the young American church to notice this element in the shadows. Puritan ministers began to praise women not only for their saintly qualities as wives and mothers, but for their pragmatic abilities. Increase Mather wrote that his mother, "a woman of singular prudence for the management of affairs, had taken off from her husband all secular cares, so that he wholly devoted himself to his study and to sacred employments."

The Great Awakening of the 1730s and 1740s not only changed religious life, it initiated an onslaught of social change, affairs that were, for the most part, managed by women. Pragmatic virtues were stressed with a fervor reminiscent of the New Testament church. Although women still had no real professional outlets and no legal status (common law assured a husband's control over his wife's assets), the church encouraged women more openly, supporting their financial and moral contributions toward the revivals of the Awakening. Women could work for the salvation of their husbands and sons on the grounds that there was "neither male nor female" in the religious community.

This spiritual rebirth pushed congregations out of their immediate worlds, and an evangelical concern took hold. As in the first century, the missionary movement gave women the opportunity to play public roles. In spite of many obstacles before the American Civil War, women organized themselves into numerous missionary societies, financing their efforts out of their household budgets. Most of their fund raising supported work directed by men. Sally Thomas (1769–1813) gave the first gift to the American Board of Commissioners for Foreign Missions. Although she received little money for her work as a housemaid, in her will she left all she possessed for missions.

Sally Thomas is an example of a great shift that seems to have occurred by this point in history—a revolutionary extension of the benevolent tradition to *all* women from *all* classes. This more democratic approach to an individual's capacity to serve is reminiscent of Christ's attitude to the poor women of the Gospels.

As doors opened for women from different financial strata, so did positions that were technically authoritative. The Civil War monopolized the efforts of the male missions directors and administrators, teachers, and theologians. Therefore, it became necessary for women to oversee the causes they had thus far only supported. For the first time, the accepted social stigmas were actively questioned, and Christian women redefined their public roles. They supported relief programs, organized fund-raising efforts for medical and devotional work among soldiers, and took charge of transportation of women and children, caring for those left vulnerable because their usual guardians were away at war. Many women supported the Abolition movement and initiated ardent campaigns against slavery. Leaders such as Harriet Beecher Stowe, Julia Ward Howe, and Sarah and Angelica Grimke provided financial support for the organized effort.

Emily Tubman (1794–1885) is a notable example of this strong spirit. From her large fortune, she gave lavishly to the church and its charities. Her efforts supported schools, educated ministers, aided evangelism, and built churches. Twenty-seven years before the Emancipation Proclamation, she freed her slaves. When sixty-nine of these people asked to be sent to Liberia, Tubman chartered a ship from Baltimore that took them to the city of Cape Palmas, Liberia. She then contributed generously to a fund that provided homes and supplies for the freed slaves arriving in Liberia from the United States. To the seventy-five who chose not to go to Liberia, Tubman gave land, clothing, and provisions until they were able to support themselves. More than many people of this period, Tubman understood the implications and responsibilities of freedom.

Postbellum benevolence
With the conclusion of the war, women continued to use the administrative skills they had acquired and invested their efforts in corporate work. Benevolent organizations fought the poverty that escalated as immigrants flocked to the cities. Similar organizations had existed in the early part of the century. Isabella Graham (1742–1814) had established the society for the Relief of Poor Widows With Small Children, and Elizabeth Seton had established the American Sisters of Charity in 1808, an organization that helped sponsor the first Catholic hospital in America.

Bishop John P. Newman called Phoebe Palmer "the Priscilla who taught many an Apollos 'the way of God more perfectly.' " No other Christian woman of the century, he believed, had exerted a comparable influence. In the area of benevolent enterprises her generosity was internationally known. She founded the Five Point Mission and provided schooling and religious training, as well as material needs for the poor. Together she and her husband seem to have conceived and made the first substantial contributions for the Chinese and the Palestinian missions.

The Salvation Army sets a stunning example of egalitarianism that blossomed during this period. Women administered and gathered funds—their leadership skills were welcomed. Catherine Booth (1829–90), the "mother" of the Salvation Army, persuasively set forth arguments for women's equality in her booklet *Female Ministry*. She was "able to hold large audiences spellbound for hours." She became one of the most famous female preachers of the time and had revolutionary ideas about money and service. Although described as being "adept at drawing large fortunes for the Army out of rich men," she never accepted profits for herself, but placed them in the treasury for the common good and used the finances to underwrite rescue houses and missions throughout the world. She once said, "Why don't you give the money and use your time for something better. Don't sit at home making other peoples' finery. Visit the sick and seek to save the lost instead."

Frances Willard (1839–78) shared the humanitarian passions of women like Catherine Booth. Willard's strong actions raised thirty thousand dollars for the first building of Garrett Biblical Institute. She also became president of Evanston College for Ladies, which later became part of Northwestern University. But she is perhaps best known as the leader of one of the greatest movements of the nineteenth century—the Temperance movement. She helped found the Women's Christian Temperance Union (WCTU), possibly the first major women's organization active around the world. These White Ribbon Missionaries often incorporated evangelism into their work with men and women from all areas of society and gave money to efforts in Asia, Africa, and South America. Willard's lectures supported not only Prohibition but also Suffrage. She believed that only women would vote for the laws that the White Ribbon Missionaries fought for. After Willard's death, WCTU members continued to raise funds for their work until 1919, when the Eighteenth Amendment established Prohibition as law.

The White Ribbon Missionaries were a component of the larger evangelical work that mushroomed among women near the end of the eighteenth century. Female missionary societies organized the "work of women for women," sending out women missionaries and supporting the schools and hospitals they established overseas.

When Mehetabel Simpkins formed "mite societies" in New England, female contributors, in the spirit of the widow in Mark 12:42–44, overwhelmed the Massachusetts Missionary Society with pennies.

Once women demonstrated that they could raise money over and above the pledges made by men, churches grew amenable to separate boards for women. The control that women wielded over the funds they raised, however, varied from denomination to denomination. But by 1880, 57 percent of the missionaries on the field were women, and the sixteen existing missionary societies had raised almost sixteen million dollars. In 1893, 60 percent of the missionaries were women, and good publicity had yielded massive fund raisers for these teachers, doctors, evangelists, and relief workers.

Charlotte (Lottie) Moon (1840–1912) is a prototype of the single female missionary of this time. This gifted, well-educated daughter of an old Virginian family could have chosen a comfortable life on her plantation home. Instead she dedicated her life to Christian service among the women of northern China, where she served for forty years. She raised the consciousness of the women of the Baptist church, and their special Christmas offerings provided relief to the Chinese plagued by starvation and diseases. They also supported other female missionaries who wanted to serve in China. Although these contributions furnished much aid, Moon, sharing the sufferings of those around her, died of starvation. In the years following her sacrifice, the Lottie Moon Christmas Offering grew to millions annually.

By 1900, there were more than forty successful women's mission societies in the United States alone. At the same time, however, as social service became professionalized, much of the control of benevolent organizations was relegated to men. Two notable exceptions were Lucy Waterbury Peabody and Helen Barrett Montgomery. For twenty years, these women worked together as ecumenical pioneers. They were involved in the founding or the early nurturing of almost every interdenominational achievement of Protestant women in America. These achievements included the World Day of Prayer, summer schools for missions, united missionary study, union schools of higher education for women overseas, and Christian literature for women and children.

Both women were strong speakers and able administrators, and inspirational for the giving public. Lucy Peabody's leadership of "College Days," the year-long campaign to finance Asian women's colleges, demonstrated her essential ability to conceive of new movements and mobilize support.

Elected president of the Northern Baptist Convention of 1921–22, Helen Montgomery became the first woman to lead a national church body. Her ability to motivate is clearly expressed in her presidential address: "We cannot continue to sing 'The Light of the World Is Jesus,' 'Jesus Shall Reign Where'er the Sun Does His Successive Journeys Run,' and contribute only our loose change to make Him King and Lord. We must either abandon our claim of His supremacy and our devotion to His cause or square our gifts with our claims."

Perhaps women like Montgomery and Peabody helped motivate young Gladys Aylward, a poor parlor maid. After three months of study in a missionary society college, she was told she was too deficient in education to become a missionary—she would never be able to learn Chinese. Thus, the committee refused her. But Aylward was sure God wanted her in China. Unable to find support, she worked as a housemaid and saved enough money for a one-way ticket to Tientsin. She left on October 15, 1932, with an old suitcase full of food, clothes, and about two pounds in English currency. Before she reached China, she had to leave the train and trudge through the snow, in bitter cold, amid gunfire from the Russo-Chinese War. When Gladys Aylward died in 1970, at the age of 68, she had had a very successful ministry among the Chinese of Yancheng, including the conversion of a local Mandarin. She spoke, read, and wrote Chinese fluently. Moreover, she had led one hundred children to safety through the mountains during the Japanese invasion and had established an orphanage.

In the late twentieth century, women continue the work of charity. Historically, their contributions to ministry and missions have affected the church far more than is generally recognized. When not allowed positions of authority, women created alternatives of service. Today, we can clearly hear the statements they made as they anointed Christ's work with their gifts—statements distinguishable even in eras when their voices were silent.

With the increasing impact of feminism and its conflicts with traditions, certain issues of authority and hierarchy will rise to the surface, and perhaps be resolved. But regardless of the outcome, the ongoing story of women and their relationship to the church tells us that the benevolent tradition will continue. Financial status and noble birth no longer play the powerful roles in determining a person's capacity for involvement, and women of all ages and classes should be able to give their money and themselves to the cause of Christ. Because more women are juggling their multifaceted commitments as professionals, wives, mothers, and individuals, new pressures and tensions may set in and shift the balance of voluntary work. If they are less able to give freely of their time, however, they will certainly find alternative, creative forms of service, using their new skills, organizing others, and supporting the charitable causes they have cherished since the time of Christ.

Reference List

Deen, Edith. *Great Women of the Christian Faith*. New York: Harper & Brothers, 1959.

Harkness, Georgia. *Women in Church and Society*. Nashville: Abingdon Press, 1972.

Hull, Gretchen Gaebelein. *Equal to Serve: Women and Men in the Church and Home*. Old Tappan, N.J.: Fleming H. Revell, 1973.

James, Janet Wilson, ed. *Women in American Religion*. Philadelphia: University of Pennsylvania, 1976.

Ruether, Rosemary, and Eleanor McLaughlin. *Women of Spirit: Female Leadership in the Jewish and Christian Tradition*. New York: Simon and Schuster, 1979.

Ruether, Rosemary Radford, and Rosemary Skinner Keller, eds. *Women & Religion in America, Vol. 3: 1900–1968. A Documentary History*. San Francisco: Harper & Row, 1986.

Tucker, Ruth A., and Walter Liefeld. *Daughters of the Church: Women and Ministry from New Testament Times to the Present.* Grand Rapids: Zondervan, 1987.

Van Scoyoc, Nancy J. *Women, Change and the Church.* Nashville: Abingdon Press, 1980.

Ward, Patricia, and Martha Stout. *Christian Women at Work.* Grand Rapids: Zondervan, 1981.

Chapter 8

WORLD HUNGER: OUR RESPONSE

Ted W. Engstrom

I n the late 1980s our world passed a significant milestone: Global population reached five billion people. When we consider that the world population was probably 250 thousand during our Lord's life on Earth, it is staggering to think that over twenty times that number of people are currently living.

Among these five billion people, about 15 percent of the world population live in absolute poverty. Absolute poverty, says the World Bank, is "a clearly defined category that represents a condition of life so characterized by malnutrition, illiteracy and disease as to be beneath any reasonable definition of human decency."

The renowned researcher on world Christianity, David Barrett, estimates that 190 million of these people living in "absolute poverty" are believers in the Lord Jesus Christ.

The poorest of the poor

Barrett also estimates that nearly half of the world (46 percent, well over two billion people) barely eke out a living in twenty-six countries, each with a per-capita income of under $225 per year. In light of such poverty and hunger, it is no wonder these Third World citizens are eagerly searching for a new world equilibrium and the creation of a more humane global society.

By the year 2000, the world population will probably be well over six billion people—perhaps as many as 6.5 billion. At the present rate of population growth, this means an increase (births over deaths) of 250,000 people daily, 1,750,000 each week, 7,000,000 each month, and 80,000,000 people per year! According to United Nations' statistics, the poorest nations will account for 90 percent of the increase. The Asian population itself will increase by 30 percent by the year 2000—from 2.8 billion to nearly 3.6 billion, which is an increase of 800 million people in a decade or less.

By the year 2000, Mexico City, now the largest city in the world with 18.5 million people, will have a population of close to 30 million people. Shanghai will have 26 million; Tokyo, 24 million; Beijing, 23 million; São Paulo, 22 million; and the New York City area, 20 million. A minimum of twenty-two cities will have populations of over 10 million by the year 2000. Urbanization already presents a tremendous challenge to all who are concerned about poverty, hunger, urban blight, and crime—as well as proclamation of our gospel message. But consider how vast will be the future problems of these cities.

As responsible Christians we must attend to the population in our megacities that are growing far more rapidly than our ability to cope with them. The exponential population growth in our cities will see major increases in crime rates and inner-city slum situations, the rise of the international drug traffic, and hosts of other serious societal problems; not least among them is the food crisis.

I have commuted to many of the nations in Africa over the past quarter of a century. I have seen serious food shortages inevitably follow years of drought and deterioration of agricultural productivity. Among the most critically affected are Chad, Ethiopia, the Sudan, Mali, Mozambique, and Mauritania.

The United Nations Food and Agricultural Organization (FAO)

indicates that the food deficiency of the twenty most seriously drought-affected African countries, including those above, in one recent year was 6.6 million metric tons of cereal grain, which is their basic diet—sorghum, millet, and maize. International relief agencies, private voluntary agencies, and U.S. government officials indicate that recent drought years have affected perhaps as many as 150 million people, and 30 million of them are in jeopardy of losing their lives.

To ignore the agonizing, genuine cry of suffering while claiming to know the Author of love is certainly unacceptable "good news" to these people. "Good news" to them must include some reason to hope that their wretched poverty is not a permanent condition for them and their future generations. In the parable of the Good Samaritan, Jesus places high priority on our love for the neglected (Luke 10:30–37). His final words in this parable are for us to "go . . . and do likewise."

In the six or more times I have visited Ethiopia, I have been amazed at the strength of the church in that troubled, Marxist-controlled nation. Many have had to go underground with their witness in recent years. The church in Ethiopia dates back to the first century when the Ethiopian eunuch was converted, as recorded in the Book of Acts. Both the ancient Coptic Church and the Ethiopian evangelical church, which has suffered so greatly from starvation, war, disease, and death, have grown apace. God's love, in the midst of indescribable suffering, has been evidenced in so many ways, and these "poorest of the poor" have witnessed by the thousands to their continuing faith in the Savior.

The silent crisis of hunger

The "hungry half" of the world consists of those people who have escaped death as babies and children, and who most often have stunted physical and mental development as well as other crippling ailments that affect their lives well past childhood. Malnutrition during a child's early years inevitably reduces both work and mental capacity. Experts tell us that formative physical development and 90 percent of the growth of the human brain occur before the age of five. These suffering, malnourished babies and little ones are the ones most seriously affected.

What some have called "the silent crisis of hunger" is the lack of energy that prohibits malnourished people from leading active and productive lives. A recent United Nations study on hunger indicated:

> Education and work, opportunities that provide the hungry with means to provide for themselves and their families, are physically out of their reach. Limited by diets that meet only the minimum requirements for survival, the hungry poor are unable to free themselves from the cycle of hunger and poverty. Low-birth-weight infants become hungry, slow-developing children who ultimately reach listless and uneducated adulthood, possess few of the human resources with which to support their families and speed the development of their countries. In this sense, hunger is a "silent" crisis that extends far beyond the more conspicuous and grotesque forms of starvation.

Chronic hunger is normally a condition of ongoing poverty. Obviously, most of the hungry are the poorest residents of the poorest communities. They often do not participate in community institutions, such as churches and schools, through which outside aid is often channeled. Merely throwing money at the problem does little good unless careful efforts are made to see that the right kind of assistance ends up in the right hands. Channeling surplus food from more prosperous nations does not attack the root cause of poverty.

The challenge is to raise incomes for the poor and provide them with access to education, as well as improve the farming techniques of the poorest producers so they can produce more food for themselves. Even though urban centers are growing at an alarming rate, the majority of the hungry today still live in agrarian-based societies. In the poorest countries, between 70 and 80 percent of all the people participate in agriculture.

To proclaim the "Good News" to starving people is not possible until we feed them; we cannot talk about heaven and eternal life to those who have no roof over their heads until we first of all meet their temporal needs; we cannot offer hope to the hopeless until we first identify with their sufferings and hurt. But what a joy it is to see the Lord take the loaves and fishes—or the cup of cold water—and again multiply them, opening the doors of opportunity for the proclamation of the gospel to those who are as hungry spiritually as they are physically.

Hungry people are real people with real feelings, real hopes, real dreams. They are not mere images on TV screens or in newspaper photos. If they seem small in our sight, it is because 40 percent of them are children. Most of the remainder are women.

Most of us will never know what it is like to be really hungry. Hunger hurts. The starving body cannibalizes itself. It consumes its own fat, muscles, and tissues. Victims become listless, confused, unable to work or think clearly. No one should have to *live* that way. More important, no one should have to *die* that way.

Satisfying the inner hunger

We have written about physical hunger. But what about the spiritual hunger underlying this condition? Just as many of the poor have reached an uneasy state of contentment with literal hunger, the average Westerner seems to be happy with a life of spiritual hunger. The society-destroying problems of substance abuse, crime, family disintegration, and endless moral decay are lost in a short-term binge of personal satisfaction.

What about the impoverished people of our world? They know they hunger for physical nourishment. Their physical hunger, however, only hides their deeper hungers. They do not feel their hunger for fellowship; they do not understand their intellectual hunger; they do not appreciate their hunger for culture and refinement. But of all the inner hungers, neither the skid row derelict, nor the bag lady, nor the street kid comprehends that greatest hunger of all, the hunger for God—the hunger to be his potential sons and daughters.

As believers in the Lord Jesus Christ, greatly blessed with all of our resources, we must continually find ways to integrate our deep concern for the physical welfare of the hungry and poor in our world with our desire that they become disciples of our Lord Jesus Christ and seekers after his kingdom and righteousness.

One of the greatest challenges in our world of hurt and suffering today is to bring a biblical program of Christian development into focus. A good working definition of Christian development is "a thoughtful attempt to assist a community to a more human existence, an existence in which there is economic, social, and spiritual self-determination. It has to do with the quality of the people's life. It means doing something with whatever is available. Development is people oriented. It seeks to help people become all that God wants them to be."

Christian development has a number of significant components:

First, Christians are people who have had a personal encounter with the Lord Jesus Christ; they know there is something more to life than bread.

Second, knowing Christ affects all areas of their lives, including the spiritual, the intellectual, and the physical.

Third, Christians see themselves as *enablers* rather than people seeking to impose something on others for their "own good." They view other men and women as having equal potential to be Spirit-filled, God-led leaders of their own societies.

Fourth, Christians share their knowledge of the gospel and give others the opportunity to accept and follow Jesus Christ while these people are being helped economically.

Finally, Christians are concerned equally with a community's move toward the Savior and with measuring its food production and health care. They measure quality of life as a spiritual dimension, picturing people as moving towards, or away from, Christ.

A major objective of development is self-reliance, though the present world systems tragically are not designed to meet that objective. The income gap is widening, and for hundreds of millions of people, self-reliance is an impossible dream. Yet we dare not settle for less. People need to support themselves. To many of them, international charity is often degrading, demeaning, and dehumanizing.

But thank God for his Word to the suffering people of ancient Israel: "I have seen the affliction of my people who are in Egypt, and have heard their cry because of their taskmasters; I know their sufferings, and I have come down to deliver them out of the hand of the Egyptians. . . . I will send you . . . that you may bring forth my people" (Exod. 3:7–8a, 10).

Many wonderfully dedicated Christians who have worked with and among oppressed peoples of the world find tremendous solace and encouragement in this lovely passage. Indeed, these words from

God greatly encourage many in Latin America who are working in the barrios. Many oppressed peoples are also encouraged when they realize that God sees, hears, and knows their affliction and suffering, and that he wishes to deliver them—usually by sending his people to help. This Scripture is as comforting to many suffering and hurting Christians as Romans 8:28 is to many of us during particular times of hardship and suffering.

Empowering the poor
Those who wish to reach hurting, hungry people for Christ must understand that God truly hears their cry for release from their modern taskmasters—that he knows their suffering and is sending people who are working toward their deliverance from oppression. To communicate the gospel and love to these people often carries a prerequisite of working to free them from the "outward" slavery that is imposed on them by others, as well as from their "inward" slavery of the sin and selfishness we all share.

Christians know the gospel is for the poor. Yet we often go to less-developed nations with all the baggage of wealthy nations. We must constantly critique our methods and our lifestyle and, by God's grace, identify with the poor as our Lord so beautifully modeled it. As difficult as that is, we must be continually aware of cultural diversity and sensitivity. For us in the West, that is not easy.

We must also acknowledge God's special concern for the power-less and our spiritual obligation to empower the poor. Commitment to such an obligation means defending the oppressed and working for their redemption and self-determination, even when this creates tension with those who hold power. We often need both to advocate their cause before the world's economic and political powers and to interpret their plight to those whom early Christians called "the followers of the Way."

Throughout Scripture, God instructs us on justice and how he restores justice to the world. Justice is retributive, repaying a person or an institution for evil deeds, but it is also saving, rescuing people from oppressive need. Justice transforms the community, so all its members are empowered to fully contribute to its God-intended *shalom*.

A World Vision paper says: "God gives Israel the law to make her just (Deut. 4:6–8). God is a 'God of justice' (Isa. 30:18). God loves (Isa. 61:8; Ps. 37:28) and does justice (Gen. 18:25; Jer. 9:24; Ps. 111:7). God demands justice of Israel in the courts (Deut. 16:20; Amos 5:15; Mic. 3:9) and in the market (Lev. 19:35–36). Where some oppress others (Isa. 1:17, 23), where the powerless need care (Jer. 7:5–6), there too God demands justice. God demands of Israel 'to do justice, and to love kindness, and to walk humbly with your God' (Mic. 6:8). God demands this justice of all the nations (Ps. 82).

"The law speaks of two sorts of justice: retributive justice and saving justice. We talk about the former in talking about contracts or crimes. We say, 'That's mine; I paid for it.' Or, 'She should get ten years in jail for doing that.' We talk about the latter when we talk about the duty to give aid. 'I couldn't let him drown!' Both are part of the justice God demands of us.

"Retributive justice is even-handed. But it is not enough to be even-handed. God pays special attention to the poor (Ps. 140:12). Since they bear the image of God, their need is a claim on justice. God expects us to be attentive in the same way (Deut. 10:12–13; Jer. 21:12; Job 29:7–17). These calls to be even-handed and to give special attention to the poor can conflict (Lev. 19:15). But there is no real conflict, and Scripture combines them in describing God:

> 'For the Lord your God is God of gods and Lord of lords, the great, the mighty, and the terrible God, who is not partial and takes no bribe. He executes justice for the fatherless and the widow, and loves the sojourner, giving him food and clothing.' (Deut. 10:17–18)"

Clearly, justice is more than simply attending to one's own affairs. The good of all is everyone's business (Job 31).

We are to live justly and seek justice, which involves both retributive and saving justice. The Old and New Testaments—and the church—provide models of this justice. Jesus gives us the New Testament; the Old Testament gives us our roots. The justice of our Lord—both retributive and saving—is the standard for our justice. Jesus is God among us, establishing the justice of his kingdom in this world. May we always, and clearly, identify with him.

From the earliest days of the New Testament church, the disciples set their hand to making sure new Christians had enough to eat.

None lacked, because they shared all things in common during those early days in Jerusalem (Acts 4:32–34). The first deacons were ordained to help streamline a "daily distribution" to widows (Acts 6:1–3), and Paul devoted a great amount of time and energy toward collecting foodstuffs from Gentiles to relieve the famine that burdened Jewish Christians in Jerusalem (1 Cor. 16:1–3).

From the earliest days, the act of relieving human hunger has played a vital role in the Christian's life. The true believer has never been allowed to accept the unacceptable. Not then. Not now. Not ever!

Chapter 9

GIVING BEYOND LEFTOVERS: STEWARDSHIP IN A CHANGING WORLD

Tom Sine

Playing Scrabble on the *Hindenburg* or rearranging deck chairs on the *Titanic*. You choose your metaphor, but the evangelical discussion of stewardship has been carried on in a closet largely cut off from our changing world or our seductive culture. Consequently, many treatments of this subject are tragically myopic, almost totally failing to engage the urgent issues of faith and society.

To participate in a serious discussion of our stewardship responsibilities as followers of Jesus Christ in a changing world, we must dramatically broaden the conversation. Most evangelical authors converse in the closet of the present, expecting the future to be an extension of what we experience now. But what is adequate in our stewardship of the immediate will not be adequate in the future.

Simply stewarding our lives and resources as we are presently doing will be totally inadequate for the challenges of tomorrow.

Not only has the conversation been limited to the closet of the present, but it has also been restricted to the closet of the private, disengaged from the larger world. Thus Christians often miss this simple truth: We live in an interdependent world in which there is no such thing as a private stewardship decision.

Finally, important discussion of stewardship has been crowded into the very small closet of practical economics. Biblical steward-ship, however, is not primarily an economic issue, but a cultural one.Unfortunately, many who write books and conduct seminars on Christian stewardship seem to accept the American culture and its priorities unquestioningly. Stewardship is reduced to rearranging the leftovers of our lives while we sail obliviously into an uncertain future.

Expanding the conversation

The eighties ended with images of young people dancing on the East Berlin wall and children in South Africa crying for freedom. Seldom have we lived in a time of such dramatic change. One leading futurist predicts we will experience as much change in the next ten years as we have in the past three decades. If his prediction is accurate, it is our responsibility as Christian stewards to anticipate the new challenges and assess how we will steward our lives and resources. Those challenges fall into three main groupings.

First, we must meet the challenge of shifting global economies. We are moving from a bipolar world, where American-Soviet dialogues have dominated communications for decades, to a multipolar world. As we enter the twenty-first century, we will see Japan, some form of a unified Germany, the European Community '92, and others aspiring to be world powers. We are likely to witness the regionalization of the global economic scene, with Japan leading the pack as the top-ranking economy in the world. It will be the center of the Asian region, which is running the highest level of economic growth of the three regions and presently growing at 5 to 10 percent a year.

European Community '92 is aspiring to see 4 to 6 percent growth annually as the second major region of the world. The third is North

America. There is little reason to believe, however, that the Canadian and American economies will even reach a 3 percent growth rate as we approach the twenty-first century. Therefore, in an increasingly competitive economic arena, North Americans will have to alter their expectations and their lifestyles.

Those who live in the Two-Thirds World will be at greatest risk. The 180 million landless poor of Asia will be left behind in the Asian liftoff. Latin America has lost ten years to the debt crisis, and every indication suggests it will lose at least another decade in trying to turn around its stagnant economies. Worst of all, the levels of economic growth and food production of Africa will not keep pace with its exploding population. The net result of these changes is that as we reach the year 2000 we will share the planet with some 6.2 billion people, and the gap between the planetary rich and poor will widen.

For that reason I wrote in *The Mustard Seed Conspiracy*, "The party is over." The great consumer society, which middle-class Americans have taken for granted, is not within the reach of hundreds of millions with whom we share this planet. They will not even survive unless we dramatically reorder our priorities for resource use. Today we share this planet with one billion people who live in a condition termed "absolute poverty"—not quite starvation, but not subsistence, either. "Absolute poverty" means making less than $90 per person per year. Half the children in this population will not reach their fifth birthday, dying of malnutrition and hunger. Meanwhile, North Americans constitute about 5 percent of the world's population, using about 40 percent of the world's resources. There is enough in the world for everyone to live decently. But there is not enough for everyone to live like middle-class Americans—not even enough for all Americans to adopt that life.

David Barrett, author of the *World Christian Encyclopedia*, tells us that of the one billion people in absolute poverty, 190 million of them are our brothers and sisters in Jesus Christ. Something is desperately wrong in the international body of Jesus Christ to have a world in which some of us are living palatially while others are unable to feed their children.

Moreover, according to Barrett's current statistics, we are actually going backwards in global evangelism as population growth outstrips our efforts at world evangelization.

Not only are we facing a world with growing spiritual and physical needs, we are also facing a future in which Earth itself is at risk. Christians must awaken to their responsibility to be stewards of God's creation. The most urgent prolife issue of the nineties will be the preservation of our planet. If we do not succeed at this, all the other prolife issues will be academic.

Second, we face the challenge of an altered American culture. The American experience will change rapidly as we approach the twenty-first century, because our society is becoming more cross-cultural. By the year 2000 in the United States, one elementary schoolchild in three will be from a minority group. If you are white and living in California in the year 2000, you will be a minority. Today the Los Angeles public-school system teaches students in sixty different languages. The culturally disadvantaged of the nineties will be middle-class white kids raised in the suburbs of America who have no cross-cultural experience, speak only one language, and do not speak that language very well. They are going to be hard pressed to live, serve, or compete in an increasingly cross-cultural future.

The church needs to rediscover its biblical commitment to be the reconciled people of God. We need to discover the gifts we have to give to one another from our African, Asian, Latin American, Hispanic, and Anglo cultures in the nineties.

In addition to becoming ethnically diverse, the American population is also rapidly growing gray. In the nineties we will see an increasing polarization between older and younger. In the sixties significant numbers of senior citizens were among the poor of America, but in the eighties, that statistic changed. Some seniors are still among the ethnic poor, but, by and large, much of the wealth of America is among seniors. They have organized politically, joining the American Association of Retired Persons and the Gray Panthers. They know how to get their way with Congress; and they vote.

The new poor of the nineties will be children—tens of thousands of children in the homeless shelters of America. The most rapidly growing segment of the homeless in the United States is children under five. Unfortunately, children neither vote nor have a political lobby. Unless evangelical compassion can range beyond the unborn child to those who have arrived—unless we can provide loving home environments for the poor and unwanted kids in our midst—there will be tremendous suffering as we approach the twenty-first century.

We have discovered that our remarkable affluence of the last eight years has not come primarily from productivity, but from borrowing. You have seen the bumper sticker "We are living off our kids' inheritance." Americans are nine trillion dollars in debt: government, corporate, and personal. We cannot borrow our affluence from the future. We are headed toward economic white water in the not-too-distant future, in which not only the poor will suffer more, but the middle class as well.

While some of the middle class are upgrading to a more affluent status, we are seeing an erosion of the bottom end of the middle class, particularly among the young. Since we have exported many of our industrial jobs overseas—jobs that used to pay $10 to $15 an hour—young people leaving high school today generally start jobs at $4 to $6 an hour. A married couple today cannot afford to live on that income, let alone think about buying a house or many of the other things the young have been programmed to want.

Third, we must face the additional challenge of finding new ways to care for the world's poor. We must discuss Christian stewardship in the context of a radically shifting world in which the global gap between rich and poor is rapidly expanding. The business-as-usual investment of time and money by the Christian community must substantially increase if we are to live faithfully in a changing world.

Western Europe has been by far the most generous sector of the world in providing assistance for the physical needs of those who live in the Two-Thirds World. Western Europe, however, will do less as it approaches the twenty-first century. At a time when Two-Thirds World assistance must dramatically increase to stimulate its economic growth, Western European countries are likely to use their limited resources to mount a mini Marshall Plan to jump-start the economies of those in Eastern Europe with whom they share borders and culture. This sharing of wealth is likely to decrease investment in the economic growth of those poorest parts of the world. The United States, due to its huge deficit, is also likely to do less in response to the urgent needs of the Two-Thirds World.

Meanwhile, in the United States, churches are experiencing a reduced commitment to giving. Mainline churches are declining and graying. According to Wade Clark Roof and William McKinney's book *America Mainline Religion*, young people are leaving mainline churches, not for conservative Protestant churches, but for secularism. With the graying and declining numbers in mainline churches, both of their witness for justice and peace and their stewardship dollars to address the physical and spiritual needs of people overseas and at home will decrease significantly.

Evangelical churches talk a great deal about world missions, but we seem to be spending more on our own expensive programs, buildings, and bureaucracies. Consequently, less money is available for fulfilling the Great Commission and the Great Commandment.

The giving patterns of young Christians, those under thirty-five, are of particular concern (see chart 3 in Appendix 2, "Facts Related to U.S. Wealth from a Global Christian Perspective"). Younger people (particularly the under twenty-five population) are giving significantly less than those who are older. According to World Vision statistics, those under twenty-five give fully 50 percent less than those who are older. We have sold young Christians the wrong dream. We have programmed them to do it all and to have it all. While their parents bought the split-level home and all the trimmings with a single income, today it takes young people at least two incomes—sometimes more. Therefore, as they go through the demographic pipeline over the next three decades, many of our Christian denominations and organizations will be at risk. These young people will not only decrease present levels of giving, they will very likely invest significantly less of their time and resources in the work of the kingdom than their parents did.

Not a private issue
Against the backdrop of this brief forecast and sobering assessment, we must ask, "What does it mean to be a faithful Christian steward in this world?"

After a thoughtful look at our international future, we must conclude that stewardship is not a private issue. It is a global issue. Every evangelical article I have read on stewardship suggests that we can buy as many things as we want—second homes, RV's, luxury cars—as long as we do not get a materialistic hang-up. But in an interdependent, interconnected world, the issue is much more than an attitude problem. If I use more than a fair share of what God has entrusted to me in my private life and congregation, someone else will go without. Let me be clear, if I simply reduce how much I spend on myself, it will do little good. But, if I invest the money or time I saved by reducing consumption to respond to the needs of others, it will guarantee that someone else will have more. There will be an automatic benefit, and we will see a dramatic increase in Christian resources being freed up to address tomorrow's urgent challenges.

Our pulpits, books, or mass media have not proclaimed that we are part of an international movement called the body of Jesus Christ, to which God has entrusted a certain amount of resources of time, education, and money. If we use more than a fair share of those resources and fail to work creatively to meet the needs of the world, others within the body of Christ will go hungry and not have the resources necessary either to proclaim or demonstrate the gospel.

Thankfully, we are seeing some Christian leaders who are not preoccupied with lifestyles of affluence, trying to play golf with the rich and famous or build expensive second homes. They are instead stewarding their lives more responsibly for the mission of God in a desperately needy world. For example, Gordon and Sherry Aeschliman, who publish *World Christian* magazine, have moved their family into a poor part of Pasadena, California, as a witness for the gospel of Jesus Christ. They have deliberately reduced their own lifestyle costs so the mission they write and talk about receives a greater share of the investment of their lives. If we can reduce the amount of money and time we spend on our own lives, we free them up for the advance of God's kingdom in response to the challenges of a world of exploding need.

Beyond the American dream

Biblical stewardship is not primarily an issue of economics, but an issue of culture and values. And yet, so many articles on stewardship expect us to adopt the values of the secular American culture as the primary commitment of our lives while stewardship is reduced to a question of how we can use the leftovers of our time and resources for the work of God. For all the talk about the lordship of Jesus, what clearly comes first for us is this: getting our careers under way;

getting our houses in the suburbs; getting our lifestyles upscaled. Stewardship is trivialized to how we can responsibly use the leftovers for God.

We cannot claim to be biblical Christians simply by living the American dream with a little Jesus overlay. The American dream is a false dream and not a biblical dream. It involves the individual pursuit of happiness, defined by visions of affluence, materialism, and status—values diametrically opposed to the values of God's kingdom.

We all want what is best for our children, but when that is co-opted by the culture, we see only what is best in economic terms. I do not think any place is harder to raise children to be Christians than in the affluent suburbs of America, where our culture's values are relentlessly forced on the young. They have to dress alike, look alike, wear the same designer clothes, and hit the ski slopes on the same weekend. But seldom does the church challenge the cultural captivity of Christians to a value system that is alien to the faith. One of the few books that does so is Donald Kraybill's book, *The Upside-Down Kingdom*. This unusual book suggests that discipleship is not Jesus working in a small, private, spiritual compartment of our hearts, helping us to think how to use our leftovers responsibly. Instead, Kraybill talks about jubilee or whole-life stewardship. He asks what would it look like if we lived out the Beatitudes. He envisions people living out the right-side-up values of the kingdom in an upside-down world.

Once we sanction the American dream as God's dream, we implicitly endorse the values of materialism, individualism, and self-seeking. Then seeking God's will becomes a very confused quest. Often when evangelicals talk about finding God's will, it is code language for figuring out how to talk God into helping us get what we want: How can I get God's help in finding a better paying job, a newer home, or even a better parking place downtown? God becomes a co-conspirator to insure that we acquire everything we want out of life without being inconvenienced. Instead, we should be co-conspirators in God's plan to change the world.

To be faithful biblical stewards, we must begin not with our pocketbooks, but with our lives, culture, and values. We must invite God's Spirit to transform not only our hearts, but our values: from lives centered on materialism to lives centered on spirituality and the worship of the living God, from lives focused on individualism to lives reconnected with communities in which we are known, loved, and held accountable. Jesus was right after all: It is only in losing life that we have hope of finding life. Only as we, like a seed, fall into the ground and die, do we have any hope of rising to something more.

Only after we have invited God to change our life direction and fundamental values—turning the other cheek, going the second mile, loving our enemies—is there any hope of our being faithful biblical stewards.

Whole-life discipleship and whole-life stewardship

The first call of the kingdom is not to proclamation or social action, but to incarnation—to clothe in flesh the right-side-up values of God's kingdom in an upside-down, fallen world. Only in community can we flesh out something of what God's kingdom looks like. Only then can we speak or act out authentically God's love in a changing world. If we put the purposes and values of God's kingdom in the center of our individual, family, and congregational lives, every-thing else will change as well. We will discover, as the Christians did in the first century, that there is no way we can claim to be followers of Christ without working for the purposes of Christ.

Christ's mission could not be clearer. In Luke 4:17–20, he stands up in the synagogue to read from Isaiah: "The Spirit of the Lord is upon me, because he has anointed me to preach good news to the poor. He has sent me to proclaim release to the captives and recovering of sight to the blind, to set at liberty those who are oppressed, to proclaim the acceptable year of the Lord." A few chapters later, John sends his disciples to learn whether Jesus is indeed Messiah. Jesus tells John's disciples, "Go and tell John what you have seen and heard: the blind receive their sight, the lame walk, lepers are cleansed, and the deaf hear, the dead are raised up, the poor have good news preached to them. And blessed is he who takes no offense at me" (Luke 7:19–20). That great tapestry of righteousness, peace, reconciliation, wholeness, and love woven into the words of the Hebrew prophets is focused in the life of a single person, the Son of God.

What it meant for him to be the true Son of God is what it means for us today: Before our occupations, our financial security, or personal interests, we must discover our vocation.

One can become a spiritual leader in any church in this country and never be expected to take any regular weekly time to be involved in service or witness to those outside the building. Fully 75 percent of the Christians in the churches I work with have no time to be involved in ministry to those beyond the doors of the church.

In the first century there was no way you could claim to be a follower of Jesus without working for the purposes of God every week. Consequently, a conversion of our values is first the transformation of our life's purposes—from lives committed to being upwardly mobile to lives committed to being outwardly caring. Every Christian, every family, must be involved in ministry.

Recently in a Presbyterian church in Bellevue, Washington, I asked, "What is it that binds the American Christian family together? Isn't it really the same as secular families: what we consume together . . . sit-com television, Big Mac hamburgers, expeditions to the shopping mall?" I have never seen a church facilitate the bonding of families in ministry to others by helping children and parents to work together every week to serve others.

I returned to that church in Bellevue some weeks later. The church had not changed, but a woman approached me and said, "We're doing it." I asked, "What are you doing?" She replied, "I'm going to homes of senior citizens who are bedfast, who will lose their homes if someone doesn't help them with their chores. I'm taking my two little preschoolers with me. They are not just watching Mom work, they are down on the floor alongside me scrubbing." What kind of children would we raise if they were involved with parents for eighteen years in service to others? The call to follow Christ is not just a call that has to do with the spiritual compartment of life. It is a call to give him all of life: "I appeal to you therefore, brethren, by the mercies of God, to present your bodies as a living sacrifice, holy and acceptable to God, which is your spiritual worship" (Rom. 12:1). It is a call to whole-life discipleship and whole-life stewardship in which the mission purposes of God—sight to the blind, release to the captives, and good news to the poor—become the orchestrating purposes of our individual and family lives. We then have the exciting opportunity to organize our family lives around God's purposes, seeking to flesh out God's values.

As God transforms our values from those of the culture to those of the kingdom, we will steward our time and money differently from those around us, not out of guilt or asceticism, but out of opportunity. We will want to be so much more a part of what God is doing.

The tithe view of stewardship customarily taught in most evangelical churches is not valid in a New Testament context. A growing number of biblical scholars tell us that the New Testament presents whole-life or jubilee stewardship, based on the premise that the Earth is the Lord's. If the Earth is indeed the Lord's, no longer is the question, How much of mine do I have to give up? but rather, How much of God's do I get to keep in a world in which there is not enough to go around, in which Christians cannot keep their kids fed, and in which we are going backward and not forward with the Great Commission? In an interdependent, interconnected world, whole-life stewardship means examining how I can responsibly use what God has entrusted to me, my family, and my congregation so it is justly shared with Christ's entire community of believers. This change must begin with our time before we can consider our finances.

I encourage individuals and couples to go on prayer retreats for a day and a half or two days at least twice a year to discern through prayer, study, and journaling how God would have them reorder their lives. How much time should they take every day for study in God's Word, prayer, and spirituality? How much time should they take for family, loved ones, and friends? How much time should they spend in a small group at least one evening a week, where they are known, loved, and held accountable; where together they seek to reflect something of the values of God's kingdom? How much time should they spend in ministry every week? Most individuals and families could, with a little creativity, find one evening a week to evangelize among international students, or work with abused kids, or work in an AIDS hospice. Children and parents together could minister to refugees or single-parent families if they committed themselves to the purposes and values of God's kingdom.

God calls us to lives with easy rhythm where we have more time for our children and celebration, but also some time for community, and—with God's help—some time to be a part of his loving intentions in a world exploding with human need. After we have created a rhythm where we have time for service, community, celebration, and our families, then it is time to look at how we steward our finances. As God transforms our values, we will use our finances differently. Belatedly we will discover consumerism, acquisition, and accumulation have nothing to do with happiness.

We must redefine the good life biblically. We will discover it has nothing to do with consumerism, but with the celebration of giving life away. We must ask the difficult but important question: "How much is enough?" In a world in which Christians cannot keep their kids fed, how much do we really need to spend on transportation, wardrobe, vacations, second homes, and RVs? In an interdependent, interconnected world we must seriously reassess how much we need to spend on our lives.

In moving from a tithe view to a whole-life view of stewardship, many people could easily give 20 to 30 percent. A doctor in Denver sold half his medical practice and supports his family very comfortably on twenty hours a week. With the other twenty hours he started an inner-city health clinic. Many people do not have to change their work style radically, but they could reduce how much they spend on housing and other activities and significantly free up a portion of either their time or money.

Six young people, who graduated from Westmont College, felt called to work for God in the inner city of Oakland, California. No one would give them any money to do that right out of college, but they could get by for about $250 per person per month for rent, food, and utilities by living cooperatively. They did not have to work full-time jobs, but took twenty-hour-a-week tentmaking jobs and lived comfortably on that income, freeing up thirty hours a week to work among the poor in Oakland. They went downtown to First Baptist Church, which had a gymnasium that had been closed for years. "Can we open the gym?" they asked. "Certainly," responded leaders at the church. After the gym was opened, forty to sixty inner-city kids immediately came off the streets. Today they have a number of ministries made possible through whole-life stewardship.

One of the top three stewardship decisions you will ever make is the decision to purchase a house. Talk all you want about the lordship of Jesus Christ, once you sign a contract for the next thirty years, you—husband and wife—are working for a mortgage company. I am not suggesting people forgo home ownership, though many Christians throughout the world will never have that opportunity. I do encourage people to be much more creative as whole-life stewards.

John and Pam saw housing as a stewardship issue. They wanted to reflect the values of God's kingdom in the way they sheltered their two sons. The first question they asked was how much floor space they really needed. Did they need a house large enough to have roller skating parties on the weekend? They decided a two-bedroom house was adequate for their family at that point.

Last year they completed the construction of a beautiful split-level, two-bedroom house. With the two bedrooms and bath upstairs, living room–dining room combination, gabled ceiling, the most beautifully crafted cabinetry I have seen in any home, and super insulation, the total cost was $25,000. What is the difference between $25,000 in cash and a $100,000-house mortgage, which is the going price in the Seattle area and really costs over a half-million dollars over thirty years? Obviously the latter represents a whole lot of two peoples' lives.

In the nineties we must be much more creative in new ways to provide shelter, particularly for Christian youth so they will be available to participate in the church tomorrow. One young pastor is trying to plant a Mennonite church in Southern California. He is struggling to find part of the answer. In the area where he is trying to plant his church, a basic three-bedroom house typically costs $250,000. He recognizes people will have very little time or money to invest helping him plant a new congregation in this area. Therefore, he wants to buy enough land to build multiplex housing instead of detached single-family housing. He hopes to start with a sixplex, in which the units will only cost $60,000 after the land is paid for. He plans to develop an interest-free mortgage strategy so young people buying these units will wind up paying $60,000 for a $60,000 house over five years instead of spending a million dollars over thirty years for a $250,000 house. The stewardship savings of time and money are self-evident. He wants to write into the contract a certain percentage of time and money that is freed up to be invested immediately in the work of God's kingdom—perhaps building

Habitat for Humanity housing in the same complex.

Before the six couples move into the sixplex, he wants them to draw up a covenant stating how they will live out the right-side-up values of the kingdom in an upside-down world. They would make a covenant as to how they will raise their children differently; how they will use resources differently; how they will celebrate life differently. Instead of being absolutely co-opted by the suburban culture around them, they will be a small example of God's kingdom, meeting one night a week to nurture and encourage one another not only in their discipleship of Jesus Christ, but in reflecting the values of God's new order and in working cooperatively in ministry to others.

In the nineties we will need tens of thousands of Christians who take this business of following Christ so seriously that they will put at the center of their lives the purposes and values of God's kingdom instead of the ambitions of the American dream. We will shelter ourselves in new ways, learning from the European community to build attached housing less expensively through alternative mortgages so we have more resources to work for God's kingdom. We will meet in communities once a week to help one another live out the right-side-up values of the kingdom in an upside-down world. We will refuse to get caught up in the stress race so we will have time not only for our children and loved ones, but also so we can be part of what God is doing to change the world. We will discover joy as we free up more of our financial resources to see God's kingdom extended throughout the world in partnership with our sisters and brothers.

The only way we can move into whole-life stewardship is to expand the conversation to what it means to be a faithful Christian disciple in a changing world and anticipate how the world is changing. We must realize that there is no such thing as a private lifestyle decision for either individuals or congregations, but that we are a part of a vast international community of believers. We must use the resources God has entrusted to us cooperatively and transnationally for the work of God's kingdom.

In addition, we must expand the conversation beyond seeing stewardship as a narrowly economic issue, understanding that God wants to change our fundamental values. If our lives come to reflect a new set of values in this fallen world, God will help us steward our resources so we can be much more a part of his loving purposes in a world that desperately needs to learn there is a God who will make all things new.

Chapter 10

THE CHRISTIAN IDEAL

Kenneth S. Kantzer

Self-indulgent materialism has seized most of Western civilization in an iron grip. In these closing years of the twentieth century, I see no real sign of any lessening of its tenacious hold upon our society. But extremes breed their opposites, and here and there in the West we hear a lonely voice raised in defense of a world-denying asceticism.

Needless to say, the self-indulgent, hedonistic variety has penetrated the nominal Christian church far more than has self-denying asceticism. But what many do not see is that both—and both equally—are the very antithesis of the way of life taught by our Lord and set forth in the Bible—in both Old and New Testaments. The self-indulgent person seeks for himself all the pleasure he can get. He—not God—is the center of his own life. And this is the essence of idolatry. The ascetic eschews vain pleasures and seeks to build the inner core of his own soul. And for him, too, he—not God—is the center of his own life. And that also is idolatry.

The Christian ideal is neither the one who seeks pleasures nor the one who denies pleasures. It is rather the one who first seeks God and his righteousness. It is to love God and to love one's neighbor. This is the key to the whole of biblical ethics (that is what our Lord said!), including the issues of wealth and poverty. Into this theme every passage of the Bible may be placed when it is properly interpreted (and I do not mean explained away).

Suiting our desires

To love God and neighbor is the key to a Christian understanding of wealth and poverty. Yet, in a fallen world, the implications of this biblical principle become exceedingly complex. Unfortunately, we tend almost irresistibly to make biblical instruction say what we would like it to say for our own personal comfort and selfish enjoyment. We seize on certain aspects of biblical teaching that suit our desires and choose to ignore or misinterpret the rest. In practice, this completely negates the clear teaching of Scripture taken as a whole.

For example, the Book of Proverbs, as well as much of the Old and New Testaments, teaches that wealth is the gift of God and a reward for obedience. Everything that exists was created by God for our good and is intended as a blessing. Even in our fallen world, God graciously gives to us good things to enjoy and graciously rewards us when we live according to the principles he built into his creation. For example, the hard-working, prudent farmer generally has better crops and makes more money. That is a true proverb intending to set forth in pithy language one isolated aspect of reality. It reflects a valid aspect of the created order and is just as true for unbelievers as for believers. Every farmer ought to be industrious and prudent. And his industry and prudence will usually have their appropriate reward. But God has not promised that locusts will never destroy the crops of either believers or unbelievers. A proverb is by no means a universal promise.

Wealth, therefore, is good, comes as a gift from God, and is often a reward for those who live in accordance with the principles he has built into the world. Yet the Bible does not teach that material wealth will come necessarily or always. God loves us too much for that. In a fallen world, it is not always best for us that God should give us material rewards; hence, because he loves us, he withholds them for our good. We plant, but drought and hail and the canker-worm destroy the crop. God permits this because he knows it is best for us.

Moreover, God calls each of his children to a particular role in life. He then gives to each what we need to fulfill this calling most effectively (or withholds what would interfere with our perform-ance). Yet he has also promised that whatever we lose for the sake of the kingdom he will make up to us either in this life or the next. So we do not ultimately lose by being obedient to his call even when that call demands some sacrifice, or even a sacrifice of our life (as is illustrated in the life of our Lord; see Phil. 2:5–11).

Of course, we must not think of God's promises to reward us merely in terms of earthly pleasures delayed until we reach heaven. There is no suggestion in the Bible of a Muslim-like heaven of sumptuous banquets served by voluptuous *houris*. The heavenly rewards promised in the Bible consist of goods that are truly good in God's sight (and, therefore, should be in our own also). They consist of a deepened relationship with God and, perhaps, with others, in the moral and spiritual character that we have formed and in the special joy that we have in serving God and pleasing him. Our reward is God himself, and is rooted in our love for him.

Letting go

Most important, wealth must never become our idol. This is the point our Lord stressed in a most radical fashion—so radically, in fact, that we try to dismiss it by ignoring or misinterpreting the message. But the teaching remains: We must give up all our wealth. We must own nothing. We are only stewards of what God owns. The point is not that we must merely be *willing* to give it up and then live like everyone else. Rather, we must actually give it up. We are to abandon completely any claims to the wealth of this world. It is not our own and we do not have ultimate control over it.

Therefore, while wealth is a gift of God and intended to be a blessing, it is never a blessing if we keep it for ourselves. As Saint

Francis taught us long ago, it is only in giving it away that we can receive it as a blessing. Even then it does not prove to be a blessing unless as God's stewards we use it in accordance with the limitations and instruction that God has given us. Of course, it must not be used selfishly, for it does not belong to us. Rather, it must be allocated by us prudently for the good of all of God's creation—especially for the care of the poor and needy. That is God's means to weld us together and to bring within the body of Christ a social and spiritual equality.

Thus, wealth is good and created by God for our good. But it is like a stick of dynamite. It may be used to build bridges or it may be used to destroy life. All wealth must be used within the moral controls for good that God has built into the universe and in which he has instructed the Christian. When these are disregarded, wealth becomes, in fact, a curse.

Wants and needs

For this reason it is especially important that we avoid luxury. But, of course, we have to ask, What is luxury? What one person considers luxury, another reckons as essential for life. It is not easy to draw a line between legitimate use of God's resources and the wasteful, luxurious use of his resources.

God invites us to enjoy his creation. He made it for us. We are to use it and enjoy it. The problem comes when we seek selfishly to use it for our own good and enjoyment apart from the equally legitimate rights of others to enjoy it. We want too much—more than is our proper share, more than is appropriate to our divinely assigned role in life, and more than we need to enable us to fulfill our divine vocation.

And how much is my need to enable me to serve God best? What is my appropriate share of the good things of this world? Of music and art and leisure and residence and car and travel? No two human beings are identical and, therefore, no two human beings have exactly the same needs even when they carry the same role in life and are called to the same tasks. This should remind us to be extraordinarily cautious in judging what our fellow Christians really need, especially when they take into their lives what, for me, would be outrageous luxury.

Each of us is a steward for God. It is our task to dispense the goods of this world in accordance with God's good pleasure and his knowledge of what is each person's fair share. This also applies to how much we allow for ourselves.

God will hold us responsible for the honesty, fairness, and unselfishness with which we make these judgments about wealth that he entrusts to us as his stewards.

A HOLY SPONTANEITY

Timothy K. Jones

Psychiatrist Karl Menninger once asked a wealthy patient, "What on earth are you going to do with all that money?" The patient replied, "Just worry about it, I suppose."

"Well, do you get that much pleasure worrying about it?" Menninger continued.

"No," responded the patient, "but I get such terror when I think about giving it to somebody."

The Bible has some strong, sometimes stringent, things to say about Mammon's unsettling power, as our contributors have shown. But alongside the warnings and the "woes to you who are rich" we read of the joyous possibility that our stance toward wealth can be rooted in spiritual certainties, that it can be brought under Christ's lordship and the Spirit's leading. Money can cease to be an idol and become a tool of blessing, where in our freedom and sharing we no longer "let [our] left hand know what [our] right hand is doing." We can uncover the apostle Paul's "secret of being content in any and every situation . . . whether living in plenty or in want" (Phil. 4:12).

It is important to close this book on such a note of possibility. A focus on the biblical principles of stewardship can leave us so weighed down with duty that we lose any delight—so burdened with obligation that we lose the spontaneous joy of serving God. The Bible instead holds out the promise that we can receive joyfully, hold lightly, and use rightly the possessions of our everyday lives.

But how? Where do we find guidance in putting scriptural principles into practice? In our day of secular investment counselors and Christian financial planners—to say nothing of books on the biblical teachings on money—what role is left for the Spirit's leading? And what role does the community of the Spirit, the church, play in our daily decisions?

Beyond control

Some years ago, I received a mailing on a life insurance program. Across the envelope was emblazoned this slogan: "Put yourself in control of your financial future." It *did* get me to read the material inside, which I suppose had morsels of sound advice, but I wondered: Is *control* of our finances and our futures the point? Does not wise planning involve something far deeper than hard-headed projections—or even sound principles?

The biblical record would certainly say so. In it we find a consistent pattern of dependence on God, not only for his provision, but also for his guidance.

This is supremely true in the New Testament, beginning with Jesus. Mennonite scholar C. Norman Kraus points out in *The Community of the Spirit* that the Pharisaism of Jesus' day had developed during a period when Jews commonly assumed that the spirit of prophecy (which had fueled the pronouncements of Isaiah or Malachi) had been withdrawn. "They had concluded that the religious community would have to be preserved by legal regulation and tradition. In the time of Jesus and the apostles, the Pharisaic community had expanded Torah into a comprehensive system of both prohibitive and prescriptive statutes. . . . Jesus found himself in sharp conflict with this scribal tradition."[1]

While he respected the "law and the prophets," Jesus placed a new accent on the providential care of a Father who numbered the hairs of our heads (Matt. 10:30), who would give the Holy Spirit to them who asked him more eagerly than a human father gives good gifts to his own children (Luke 11:11–13), and who would send the Spirit to guide his children "into all truth" (John 16:13). The new community was to be constituted not by a new law, but by God's action in Christ, and Christ's continuing presence through the Spirit. This Spirit would lead the church and work out God's purposes through its members. "The Counselor," Jesus promised, "the Holy Spirit, whom the Father will send in my name, will teach you all things and will remind you of everything I have said to you" (John 14:26).

This attitude could not help affecting the early church's attitude toward material matters. "No one claimed that any of his possessions were his own, but they shared everything they had. . . . There were no needy persons among them" (Acts 4:32, 34a). Such a practice was based not on principles or some rigid legal code. Rather, it came about as the early church's response to the apostles' teaching and the Spirit's leading. "With great power the apostles continued to testify to the resurrection of the Lord Jesus, and much grace was upon them all" (Acts 4:33). This overwhelming assurance of God's sovereignty, the resurrection's reality, and the Spirit's guiding power allowed the early church to have a holy, almost reckless, spontaneity. These Christians were secure in God's care to provide, as well as in his ability to lead.

This conviction assumed an intensely practical side when, in Acts 6:1–7, the early church discovered that the Greek-speaking widows among them had been neglected in the daily distribution of food. The apostles chose seven men who were "known to be full of the Holy Spirit and wisdom." They wanted individuals not only with practical know-how, but also wisdom born of sitting at the apostles' feet and discernment in matters that required the Spirit's leading.

Paul himself was clear about the spiritual dimension of rightly using and freely sharing possessions. While his epistles were filled with ethically practical injunctions, he rarely gave direction without first establishing the theological and spiritual certainties behind them.

He told the church at Galatia, for instance, not to grow weary in well-doing (Gal. 6:9), but only after reminding them that they must "live by the Spirit," not the sinful nature (5:16), and admonishing them that "since we live by the Spirit, let us keep in step with the Spirit" (5:25). And he told the Corinthian Christians to "finish the work" of the offering for the Macedonian Christians only after repeating his recital of "the grace of our Lord Jesus Christ, [who] though he was rich, yet for our sakes became poor" (2 Cor. 8:9, 11). If they were to give "not reluctantly" and cheerfully, it was because "God is able to make all grace abound . . . so that in all things at all times, having all that [they] need, [they could] abound in every good work. . . . [being made] generous on every occasion" (2 Cor. 9:7, 8, 11). Paul even lists giving as a spiritual gift in Romans 12:8.

The Bible, particularly the New Testament, emphasizes a spiritual dimension to money and possessions that allows us to be unfettered and generous, and therefore free to respond to needs as the Spirit leads.

The history of the church is rich with stories of those who found this freedom. Francis of Assisi and his followers braved physical impoverishment and scorn from friends because a childlike, almost whimsical approach to faith lifted them above anxiety. Francis would often give away whatever clothing he had, so filled was he with effervescent joy that he seemed oblivious to want. J. Hudson Taylor launched a great chapter in missions history known as the China Inland Mission because he refused to let his meager resources determine whether or not he would go, trusting that God would both lead and supply. George Müller, nineteenth-century minister and orphanage founder, housed and fed thousands of homeless children, announcing his financial needs to no one but God. Such an approach, he would later write, "has been the means of letting us see the tender love and care of God over his children, even in the most minute things." Such examples are simply some of the best-known or most-remembered; they represent untold numbers of other believers.

Richard Foster tells a contemporary story of how the Spirit can not only free us, but guide us in the use of our possessions: "I was preparing for a weekend trip that involved speaking at three different churches. The financial arrangement was for each church to take up a little offering on my behalf when I had finished speaking. As I was meditating on what God desired of me for that weekend, I had the strong impression that I was not to take any money at all from these churches. . . .

"I told the pastors of the first two churches that any offering should be given to the poor or disposed of in whatever way they saw fit. Although surprised at my unorthodox request, they were congenial to the idea. But I arrived at the third church just as the service began, and so had no opportunity to explain my concern. I was relieved, however, when they did not take up an offering for me, and assumed that the matter was settled.

"It was late when I finally arrived at the home where I was to spend the night. As I walked in the door my host handed me a check of an amount that was, for me, considerable. It was from the church. I protested, but they mistook my concern for modesty and insisted with such vigor that I let the matter drop.

"I wish I could express . . . the experience I went through that night. There was the check lying on the nightstand, mine to take. I did not want to cause offense or seem ungrateful; after all, the money had been given for me. Maybe this last church should be considered an experience separate from the others. But what about the earlier directive—it had seemed quite clear. Back and forth it went. Finally, I had about decided that I really should take the money rather than cause any trouble, but I was determined to review my decision once more in the morning when I was rested. I invited God to teach me while I slept if he desired.

"When I opened my eyes the next morning it was unmistakably clear to me that I could not—must not—take the money. . . . With considerable trepidation I explained to my hosts why I could not take the gracious gift. The moment I finished there rushed into me an unspeakable joy. Though outwardly I tried to remain calm, I was being filled with an overwhelming sense of the glory of God. Once alone in the car I shouted and sang and blessed God. I did not have to be controlled by money! . . . It was wonderful, jubilant ecstasy. . . . (I was pleased to learn later that the church decided to give the money for refugee work in Cambodia.)"[2]

A look at practicalities

If God can free us and bring guidance to our use of money, how can we know and follow his leading? How can we give priority to the spiritual dimension of wealth and sharing in concrete ways?

First, we can continue to soak ourselves in the Bible's sometimes soothing, sometimes unsettling words about trust. Some may find it helpful to read relevant passages with a highlighting marker in hand, noting verses that speak with special force.

We should not only read, but *absorb* passages that call us, for example, to consider the lilies of the field and the birds of the air (Matt. 6). We may want to memorize verses that remind us that as we seek first the kingdom, "all these things will be given" as well (Matt. 6:34). Paul's word to the Philippians that they "not be anxious about anything" may provide good material for prayerful meditation as we wait in line at the supermarket checkout or take a hike in the woods. We may need to bring our spending and giving patterns under the careful scrutiny of passages about tithing, or laying up treasures in heaven. The same Spirit who guided the inspiration of Scripture wants to guide our lives today.

Second, we need to make our finances a matter of regular prayer. How often do we make our large purchases an agenda item for our quiet times? Do we seek God's guidance by opening our consciences to his still, small voice? Do we *ask* for help and guidance on a regular basis? Do we pray for greater trust and open-handed generosity? We can count on God's eagerness to answer such prayers.

Third, we sometimes need the guiding wisdom of other believers. No one of us is wise enough, "spiritual" enough, and generous enough to make our finances an entirely private matter. We need to talk with our spouses, friends, perhaps even our pastors, to invite their insight and enlist their prayerful seeking. Home study or "cell" groups that invite members to share personal struggles or joys may help.

Such community of support and help for our growth in stewardship can be found in many ways, and it need not always be formal or involve a large amount of time. A brown-bag lunch with colleagues or a tennis match with a friend could be the occasion to benefit from another's wise counsel.

Finally, we can experience freedom in Christ under the Spirit's leading by simply *giving*, even when our finances seem tight.

My wife and I have gone through a number of times of financial stringency in our married life. But how often have we discovered that when we give—anyway—we experience lightness and joy. The mentality of want and poverty that begins to tighten all aspects of our life—our relationships with our children, our attitude toward the future—is broken by the simple act of giving. When we have acted on the Spirit's leading—as he speaks through Scripture, our listening prayers, and our consciences—we discover a resulting freedom worth far more to us than any amount we might save by our withholding.

Glimpses of liberation

Whatever the place for concrete steps and practical disciplines, cultivating holy spontaneity around money and possessions has more to do with the inner life than it does with outer practice. A light-handed approach to the "things" of everyday life comes ultimately from a vision of spiritual realities. The Spirit brings us not to new regulations, but to glimpses of our liberation in Christ from Mammon's bondage.

This was certainly Paul's conviction as he wrote his letter to the church at Rome. Tensions were mounting there between gentile and Jewish Christians, in part over the observance of kosher dietary laws. When it came to these food regulations, some well-intentioned believers were not clear about what it meant to have freedom in Christ. Paul knew, however, that the Christian life can never be reduced to stifling lists of how-to's and don't-do's. "The kingdom of God," he wrote, "is not a matter of eating and drinking, but of righteousness, peace and joy in the Holy Spirit" (Rom. 14:17).

Serving the Lord with our pocketbooks and our budgets, then, can never be a matter of nitpicking over the details of practice. Even the clear guideline in Scripture about tithing, for example, should never become a harsh taskmaster. There can be—should be—a certain sense of joy, even amid the sacrifices to which God may call us as we follow his leading in our finances.

Years ago, when my wife and I were looking ahead and budgeting for my last year in seminary, we had a baby due (whose prenatal care and delivery were not covered by student medical insurance), to say nothing of grad school bills. As we planned, we placed our projected expenses alongside our projected income. The latter fell just short—*before* we figured in our tithe. We resolved to give 10 percent anyway—haltingly, to be sure, but also joyfully, convinced God was calling us to the discipline and delight of this ancient standard. Our joy was multiplied when we finished the year with a bit of money to spare.

Members of religious traditions that make tithing a legalistic requirement sometimes have to rediscover the joy of giving. A friend from such a tradition, taught from youth that the tithe must always go in its entirety to the local church, is finding the Spirit giving him a new latitude when it comes to his offerings. While he tithes faithfully, he has discovered the joy of sharing portions of his tithe, as the Spirit leads, with needy people or ministries and agencies not always included in his church's budgets and benevolences.

My friend knows he still has a ways to go when it comes to wealth and generosity. But his attitude toward the generosity yet to grow and flourish within him is shot through with grace. "The Spirit has not chosen to perfect all of me at once," he reflects. "Sometimes he works on my materialism, other times my anger, still other times my pride. But he seems to have pity on me not to try to change everything within at once."

That is a hopeful word for us, as well, as we ponder all the challenges and changes reading this book may prompt. As we are willing, or even *wanting* to be willing, God will guide, comfort, and bring us to a new place of freedom.

Mammon need never hold us in the jaws of the "Midas trap." Money's power to control us will inevitably lose its grip as we open our lives to the Spirit's power. As we learn to manage money, not be mastered by it, we can count on God's gracious help.

Notes

1. C. Norman Kraus, *The Community of the Spirit* (Grand Rapids: Eerdmans, 1974), 22.

2. Richard J. Foster, *Freedom of Simplicity* (San Francisco: Harper & Row, 1981), 106–7.

THE OXFORD DECLARATION ON CHRISTIAN FAITH AND ECONOMICS

Introduction by W. Ward Gasque

In the old days, Christians used to anathematize one another for theological heresies; some issues represented truly significant matters, others were seemingly trivial.

Today, most believers tend to treat one another with greater respect, giving the other the benefit of the theological doubt. And even when there are significant theological differences among them, they usually part company amicably.

The unfortunate exceptions today seem to be in the areas of politics and economics, where the debate remains heated, frequently leading to harsh words, if not violent actions, against Christians who may hold the same evangelical theology but who take different stances on economic issues. Brothers and sisters in Christ, who are united in doctrine, anathematize one another—or at least write scathing reviews, essays, and books against the alleged views of those on "the other side." Meanwhile, they respond to the criticisms aimed at their position by declaring that their opponents simply do not understand the facts or that they have totally misinterpreted their position.

The Oxford Conference on Christian Faith and Economics grew out of the conviction that this impasse between "the Christian Left" and "the Christian Right" (and a variety of perspectives in between) was both detrimental to the cause of Christ and a hindrance to clear, Christian thinking. Common commitment to Jesus as Lord and involvement in his body, the church, demands a seeking of his will on such an important aspect of life that touches all of us. It also demands that we learn to listen to one another as we seek clarification of complicated issues.

In January 1987, a small cadre of evangelical theologians, economists, missionaries, business people, and other professionals gathered together at the newly founded, Third-World-focused Oxford Centre for Mission Studies in Oxford, England, for a week of discussion of contemporary economic issues. The goal was to delineate principles that were both faithful to the Bible and grounded in contemporary economic analysis—principles that offer guidelines while overcoming the divisions that so often mark Christians as they address the subject.

A brief and fairly limited statement of agreement, along with other papers that had been read at the conference, was published in the journal *Transformation* (4[1987], 3/4). Conferees also agreed at that time that a much larger group, representing the whole range of the church and evangelical Christian opinion, be invited together for a detailed study of the subject for a period of three years. Regional groups around the world would research and reflect on the issue, and these groups would comprise theologians, business people, government workers, missionaries, academics, and laypersons—in short, a truly representative group of world Christian leadership.

A number of crucial issues were to be addressed under the headings of (1) "Creation and Stewardship," (2) "Work and Leisure," (3) "Poverty and Justice," and (4) "Freedom, Government, and Economics." A major research project was also suggested on the possible impact of the development of grassroots micro-economic projects on the pressing problem of world poverty.

Three years later, during January 1990, a much larger group spent six days together, collecting some of the conclusions of the three-year study. At this conference nearly 130 people from 37 countries attended. And what an impressive group they were!

It would have been hard to imagine a more diverse group of people coming together anywhere outside of a United Nations–sponsored conference. Millionaire business people sitting down with Latin American liberation theologians; Third World government officials in dialogue with representatives of conservative think tanks; grass-roots development workers in conversation with international bankers; academic economists listening to social workers; Bible scholars learning from international statespeople—all recognizing the lordship of Jesus Christ over the whole of life, and each attempting to listen to other brothers and sisters who represented different perspectives and experiences.

At the beginning of the week, a great deal of skepticism was expressed about the possibility of our coming to a common understanding on the subject. There was such a vast array of ideological differences manifest. How could we possibly come to agree on anything concerning economics when we did not speak the same language—in some cases literally, and in other cases figuratively? Moreover, how could those who had recently joined the discussion catch up with those who had been in dialogue for three years?

"With men this is impossible, but with God all things are possible," to quote the words of our Lord (Matt. 19:26b). To our surprise, as we met daily for Bible study and prayer, as we learned to trust one another, listening sympathetically to each other as we worshiped and prayed together, we found there were many things we could agree on.

We brought many differences, and many of these remained; but as views were clarified, many assumed differences seemed to disappear. As issues were discussed and new light came to be shed on a variety of subjects, most of the participants found that some of their previously held views were actually changed. And as fellow Christians came to trust one another more deeply, they were more open to learn from each other's insights and life experiences, to value and to respect their differences rather than be threatened by them.

It would be misleading to say there was a total meeting of the minds at the conference, but there was certainly a meeting of the hearts and spirits of those who participated. Thorny issues were most definitely clarified.

Some would have liked to have seen a clear assertion in the declaration that capitalism is as corrupt and anti-Christian an economic-political system as communism, while others would have liked to have seen a more positive and explicit affirmation of capitalism as God's "more excellent way" out of the current world economic dilemma. But there was much joy taken in the fact that we were able to reach general agreement on many other important issues.

"The Oxford Declaration on Christian Faith and Economics" is not the last word on economics from a biblical Christian perspective, but it certainly is an important first or second word. It should provide serious students of both political economics and the Bible with much food for thought as they seek to bring the spiritual and physical realms of reality of life together. A great deal more work is needed. If this document makes an impact upon the world evangelical community similar to that made by the Lausanne Covenant over the past decade, a large section of the world economy will be changed for the better.

The Oxford Declaration on Christian Faith and Economics

Preamble

This Oxford Declaration on Christian Faith and Economics of January, 1990 is issued jointly by over one hundred theologians and economists, ethicists and development practitioners, church leaders and business managers who come from various parts of the world. We live in diverse cultures and subcultures, are steeped in differing traditions of theological and economic thinking, and therefore have diverse notions as to how Christian faith and economic realities should intersect. We have found this diversity enriching even when we could not reach agreement. At the same time we rejoice over the extent of unanimity on the complex economics of today made possible by our common profession of faith in our Lord Jesus Christ.

We affirm that through his life, death, resurrection, and ascension to glory, Christ has made us one people (Gal. 3:28). Though living in different cultures, we acknowledge together that there is one body and one Spirit, just as we are called to the one hope, one Lord, one faith, one baptism, and one God and Father of us all (Eph. 4:4).

We acknowledge that a Christian search for truth is both a communal and also an individual effort. As part of the one people in Christ, each of us wants to comprehend the relevance of Christ to the great issues facing humanity today together "with all the saints" (Eph. 3:18). All our individual insights need to be corrected by the perspectives of the global Christian community as well as Christians through the centuries.

We affirm that Scripture, the word of the living and true God, is our supreme authority in all matters of faith and conduct. Hence we turn to Scripture as our reliable guide in reflection on issues concerning economic, social, and political life. As economists and theologians, we desire to submit both theory and practice to the bar of Scripture.

Together we profess that God, the sovereign of life, in love made a perfect world for human beings created to live in fellowship with God. Although our greatest duty is to honour and glorify God, we rebelled against God, fell from our previous harmonious relationship with God, and brought evil upon ourselves and God's world. But God did not give up on the creation. As Creator, God continues patiently working to overcome the evil which was perverting the creation. The central act of God's redemptive new creation is the death, resurrection and reign in glory of Jesus Christ, the Son of God, and the sending of the Holy Spirit. This restoration will only be completed at the end of human history and the reconciliation of all things.

Justice is basic to Christian perspectives on economic life. Justice is rooted in the character of God. "For the Lord is righteous, he loves justice." (Ps. 11:7) Justice expresses God's actions to restore God's provision to those who have been deprived and to punish those who have violated God's standards.

A. CREATION AND STEWARDSHIP

God the Creator

1. From God and through God and to God are all things (Rom. 11:36). In the freedom of God's eternal love, by the word of God's omnipotent power, and through the Creator Spirit, the Triune God gave being to the world and to human beings which live in it. God pronounced the whole creation good. For its continuing existence creation is dependent on God. The same God who created it is present in it, sustaining it and giving it bountiful life (Ps. 104:29). In Christ, "all things were created ... and all things hold together" (Col. 1:15–20). Though creation owes its being to God, it is itself not divine. The greatness of creation—both human and non-human—exists to glorify its Creator. The divine origin of the creation, its continued existence through God, redemption through Christ, and its purpose to glorify God are fundamental truths which must guide all Christian reflection on creation and stewardship.

Stewardship of creation

2. God the Creator and Redeemer is the ultimate owner. "The earth is the Lord's and the fullness thereof" (Ps. 24:1). But God has entrusted the earth to human beings to be responsible for it on God's behalf. They should work as God's stewards in the creative, faithful management of the world, recognizing that they are responsible to God for all they do with the world and to the world.

3. God created the world and pronounced it "very good" (Gen. 1:31). Because of the Fall and the resulting curse, creation "groans in travail" (Rom. 8:22). The thoughtlessness, greed, and violence of sinful human beings have damaged God's good creation and produced a variety of ecological problems and conflicts. When we abuse and pollute creation, as we are doing in many instances, we are poor stewards and invite disaster in both local and global eco-systems.

4. Much of human aggression toward creation stems from a false understanding of the nature of creation and the human role in it. Humanity has constantly been confronted by the two challenges of selfish individualism, which neglects human community, and rigid

collectivism, which stifles human freedom. Christians and others have often pointed out both dangers. But only recently have we realised that both ideologies have a view of the world with humanity at the centre, which reduces material creation to a mere instrument.

5. Biblical life and world view is not centred on humanity. It is God-centred. Non-human creation was not made exclusively for human beings. We are repeatedly told in the Scripture that all things—human beings and the environment in which they live—were "for God" (Rom. 11:36; 1 Cor. 8:6; Col. 1:16). Correspondingly, nature is not merely the raw material for human activity. Though only human beings have been made in the image of God, non-human creation too has a dignity of its own, so much so that after the flood God established a covenant not only with Noah and his descendants, but also "with every living creature that is with you" (Gen. 9:9). Similarly, the Christian hope for the future also includes creation. "The creation itself will be set free from its bondage to decay and obtain the glorious liberty of the children of God" (Rom. 8:21).

6. The dominion God gave human beings over creation (Gen. 1:30) does not give them licence to abuse creation. First, they are responsible to God, in whose image they were made, not to ravish creation but to sustain it, as God sustains it in divine providential care. Second, since human beings are created in the image of God for community and not simply as isolated individuals (Gen. 1:28), they are to exercise dominion in a way that is responsible to the needs of the total human family, including future generations.

7. Human beings are both part of creation and also unique. Only human beings are created in the image of God. God thus grants human beings dominion over the non-human creation (Gen. 1:28–30). But dominion is not domination. According to Genesis 2:15, human dominion over creation consists in the twofold task of "tilling and taking care" of the garden. Therefore, all work must have not only a productive but also a protective aspect. Economic systems must be shaped so that a healthy ecological system is maintained over time. All responsible human work done by the

stewards of God the Sustainer must contain an element of cooperation with the environment.

Stewardship and economic production

8. Economic production results from the stewardship of the earth,
which God assigned to humanity. While materialism, injustice, and
greed are in fundamental conflict with the teaching of the whole
scripture, there is nothing in Christian faith that suggests that the
production of new goods and services is undesirable. Indeed, we are
explicitly told that God "richly furnishes us with everything to
enjoy" (1 Tim. 6:17). Production is not only necessary to sustain life
and make it enjoyable; it also provides an opportunity for human
beings to express their creativity in the service of others. In assessing
economic systems from a Christian perspective, we must consider
their ability both to generate and to distribute wealth and income
justly.

Technology and its limitations

9. Technology mirrors the basic paradox of the sinfulness and
goodness of human nature. Many current ecological problems result
from the extensive use of technology after the onset of industrializa-
tion. Though technology has liberated human beings from some
debasing forms of work, it has also often dehumanised other forms
of work. Powerful nations and corporations that control modern
technology are regularly tempted to use it to dominate the weak for
their own narrow self-interest. As we vigorously criticise the negative effects of technology, we should, however, not forget its positive
effects. Human creativity is expressed in the designing of tools for
celebration and work. Technology helps us meet the basic needs of
the world population and do so in ways which develop the creative
potential of individuals and societies. Technology can also help us
reverse environmental devastation. A radical rejection of modern
technology is unrealistic. Instead we must search for ways to use
appropriate technology responsibly according to every cultural
context.

10. What is technologically possible is not necessarily morally
permissible. We must not allow technological development to fol-

low its own inner logic, but must direct it to serve moral ends. We acknowledge our limits in foreseeing the impact of technological change and encourage an attitude of humility with respect to technological innovation. Therefore, continuing evaluation of the impact of technological change is essential. Four criteria derived from Christian faith help us to evaluate the development and use of technology. First, technology should not foster disintegration of family or community, or function as an instrument of social domination. Second, persons created in the image of God must not become mere accessories of machines. Third, as God's stewards, we must not allow technology to abuse creation. If human work is to be done in cooperation with creation then the instruments of work must cooperate with it too. Finally, we should not allow technological advancements to become objects of false worship or seduce us away from dependence on God (Gen. 11:1–9). We may differ in the weight we ascribe to individual criteria in concrete situations and therefore our assessment of particular technologies may differ. But we believe that these criteria need to be taken into consideration as we reflect theologically on technological progress.

11. We urge individuals, private institutions, and governments everywhere to consider both the local, immediate, and the global, long term ecological consequences of their actions. We encourage corporate action to make products which are more "environmentally friendly". And we call on governments to create and enforce just frameworks of incentives and penalties that will encourage both individuals and corporations to adopt ecologically sound practices.

12. We need greater international cooperation between individuals, private organisations, and nations to promote environmentally responsible action. Since political action usually serves the self-interest of the powerful, it will be especially important to guarantee that international environmental agreements are particularly concerned to protect the needs of the poor. We call on Christians everywhere to place high priority on restoring and maintaining the integrity of creation.

B. WORK AND LEISURE

Work and human nature

13. Work involves all those activities done, not for their own sake, but to satisfy human needs. Work belongs to the very purpose for which God originally made human beings. In Genesis 1:26–28, we read that God created human beings in his image "in order to have dominion over . . . all the earth". Similarly, Genesis 2:15 tells us that God created Adam and placed him in the garden of Eden to work in it, to "till it and keep it". As human beings fulfil this mandate, they glorify God. Though fallen, as human beings "go forth to their work," they fulfil an original purpose of the Creator for human existence.

14. Because work is central to the Creator's intention for humanity, work has intrinsic value. Thus work is not solely a means to an end. It is not simply a chore to be endured for the sake of satisfying human desires or needs, especially the consumption of goods. At the same time, we have to guard against over-valuation of work. The essence of human beings consists in that they are made in the image of God. Their ultimate, but not exclusive, source of meaning and identity does not lie in work, but in becoming children of God by one Spirit through faith in Jesus Christ.

15. For Christians, work acquires a new dimension. God calls all Christians to employ through work the various gifts that God has given them. God calls people to enter the kingdom of God and to live a life in accordance with its demands. When people respond to the call of God, God enables them to bear the fruit of the Spirit and endows them individually with multiple gifts of the Spirit. As those who are gifted by the Spirit and whose actions are guided by the demands of love, Christians should do their work in the service of God and humanity.

The purpose of work

16. In the Bible and in the first centuries of the Christian tradition, meeting one's needs and the needs of one's community (especially its underprivileged members) was an essential purpose of work (Ps.

128:2; 2 Thess. 3:8; 1 Thess. 4:9–12; Eph. 4:28; Acts 20:33–35). The first thing at issue in all fields of human work is the need of human beings to earn their daily bread and a little more.

17. The deepest meaning of human work is that the almighty God established human work as a means to accomplish God's work in the world. Human beings remain dependent on God, for "unless the Lord builds the house, those who build it labour in vain" (Ps. 127:1a). As Genesis 2:5 suggests, God and human beings are co-labourers in the task of preserving creation.

18. Human work has consequences that go beyond the preservation of creation to the anticipation of the eschatological transformation of the world. They are, of course, not ushering in the kingdom of God, building the "new heavens and a new earth." Only God can do that. Yet their work makes a small and imperfect contribution to it—for example, by shaping the personalities of the citizens of the eternal kingdom that will come through God's action alone.

19. However, work is not only a means through which the glory of human beings as God's stewards shines forth. It is also a place where the misery of human beings as impeders of God's purposes becomes visible. Like the test of fire, God's judgment will bring to light the work that has ultimate significance because it was done in cooperation with God. But it will also manifest the ultimate insignificance of work done in cooperation with those evil powers which scheme to ruin God's good creation (1 Cor. 3:12–15).

Alienation in work
20. Sin makes work an ambiguous reality. It is both a noble expression of human creation in the image of God, and, because of the curse, a painful testimony to human estrangement from God. Whether human beings are tilling the soil in agrarian societies, or operating high-tech machinery in information societies, they work under the shadow of death, and experience struggle and frustration in work (Gen. 3:17–19).

21. Human beings are created by God as persons endowed with gifts which God calls them to exercise freely. As a fundamental dimen-

sion of human existence, work is a personal activity. People should never be treated in their work as mere means. We must resist the tendency to treat workers merely as costs of labour inputs, a tendency evident in both rural and urban societies, but especially where industrial and post-industrial methods of production are applied. We encourage efforts to establish managerial and technological conditions that enable workers to participate meaningfully in significant decision-making processes, and to create opportunities for individual development by designing positions that challenge them to develop their potential and by instituting educational programs.

22. God gives talents to individuals for the benefit of the whole community. Human work should be a contribution to the common good (Eph. 4:28). The modern drift from concern for community to preoccupation with self, supported by powerful structural and cultural forces, shapes the way we work. Individual self-interest can legitimately be pursued, but only in a context marked by the pursuit of the good of others. These two pursuits are complementary. In order to make the pursuit of the common good possible, Christians need to seek to change both the attitudes of workers and the structures in which they work.

23. Discrimination in work continues to oppress people, especially women and marginalised groups. Because of race and gender, people are often pushed into a narrow range of occupations which are often underpaid, offer little status or security, and provide few promotional opportunities and fringe benefits. Women and men and people of all races are equal before God and should, therefore, be recognised and treated with equal justice and dignity in social and economic life.

24. For most people work is an arduous good. Many workers suffer greatly under the burden of work. In some situations people work long hours for low pay, working conditions are appalling, contracts are non-existent, sexual harassment occurs, trade union representation is not allowed, health and safety regulations are flouted. These things occur throughout the world whatever the economic system.

The word "exploitation" has a strong and immediate meaning in such situations. The God of the Bible condemns exploitation and oppression. God's liberation of the Israelites from their oppression served as a paradigm of how God's people should behave towards workers in their midst (Lev. 25:39–55).

25. Since work is central to God's purpose for humanity, people everywhere have both the obligation and the right to work. Given the broad definition of work suggested above (cf. Para. 13), the right to work here should be understood as part of the freedom of the individual to contribute to the satisfaction of the needs of the community. It is a freedom right, since work in its widest sense is a form of self-expression. The right involved is the right of the worker to work unhindered. The obligation is on every human being to contribute to the community. It is in this sense that Paul says, "if a man will not work, let him not eat."

26. The right to earn a living would be a positive or sustenance right. Such a right implies the obligation of the community to provide employment opportunities. Employment cannot be guaranteed where rights conflict and resources may be inadequate. However the fact that such a right cannot be enforced does not detract in any way from the obligation to seek the highest level of employment which is consistent with justice and the availability of resources.

Rest and leisure

27. As the Sabbath commandment indicates, the Biblical concept of rest should not be confused with the modern concept of leisure. Leisure consists of activities that are ends in themselves and therefore intrinsically enjoyable. In many parts of the world for many people, life is "all work and no play". While masses of people are unemployed and thus have only "leisure", millions of people—including children—are often overworked simply to meet their basic survival needs. Meanwhile, especially in economically developed nations, many overwork to satisfy their desire for status.

28. The first pages of the Bible tell us that God rested after creating the universe (Gen. 2:2–3). The sequence of work and rest that we see

in God's activity is a pattern for human beings. In that the Sabbath commandment interrupted work with regular periods of rest, it liberates human beings from enslavement to work. The Sabbath erects a fence around human productive activity and serves to protect both human and non-human creation. Human beings have, therefore, both a right and an obligation to rest.

29. Corresponding to the four basic relations in which all people stand (in relationship to non-human creation, to themselves, to other human beings, and to God), there are four activities which we should cultivate in leisure time. Rest consists in the enjoyment of nature as God's creation, in the free exercise and development of abilities which God has given to each person, in the cultivation of fellowship with one another, and above all, in delight in communion with God.

30. Worship is central to the Biblical concept of rest. In order to be truly who they are, human beings need periodic moments of time in which God's commands concerning their work will recede from the forefront of their consciousness as they adore the God of loving holiness and thank the God of holy love.

31. Those who cannot meet their basic needs without having to forgo leisure can be encouraged by the reality of their right to rest. The right to rest implies the corresponding right to sustenance for all those who are willing to work "six days a week" (Exod. 20:9). Modern workaholics whose infatuation with status relegates leisure to insignificance must be challenged by the liberating obligation to rest. What does it profit them to "gain the whole world" if they "forfeit their life" (Mark 8:36)?

C. POVERTY AND JUSTICE

God and the poor

32. Poverty was not part of God's original creation, nor will poverty be part of God's restored creation when Christ returns. Involuntary poverty in all its forms and manifestations is a result of the fall and its consequences. Today one of every five human beings lives in poverty so extreme that their survival is daily in doubt. We believe this is offensive and heart breaking to God.

33. We understand that the God of the Bible is one who in mercy extends love to all. At the same time, we believe that when the poor are oppressed, God is the "defender of the poor" (Ps. 146:7-9). Again and again in every part of scripture, the Bible expresses God's concern for justice for the poor. Faithful obedience requires that we share God's concern and act on it. "He who oppresses a poor man insults his maker, but he who is kind to the needy honours Him" (Prov. 14:31). Indeed it is only when we right such injustices that God promises to hear our prayers and worship (Isa. 58:1-9).

34. Neglect of the poor often flows from greed. Furthermore, the obsessive or careless pursuit of material goods is one of the most destructive idolatries in human history (Eph. 5:5). It distracts individuals from their duties before God, and corrupts personal and social relationships.

Causes of poverty

35. The causes of poverty are many and complex. They include the evil that people do to each other, to themselves, and to their environment. The causes of poverty also include the cultural attitudes and actions taken by social, economic, political and religious institutions, that either devalue or waste resources, that erect barriers to economic production, or that fail to reward work fairly. Furthermore, the forces that cause and perpetuate poverty operate at global, national, local, and personal levels. It is also true that a person may be poor because of sickness, mental or physical handicap, childhood, or old age. Poverty is also caused by natural disasters such as earthquakes, hurricanes, floods, and famines.

36. We recognise that poverty results from and is sustained by both constraints on the production of wealth and on the inequitable distribution of wealth and income. We acknowledge the tendency we have had to reduce the causes of poverty to one at the expense of the other. We affirm the need to analyse and explain the conditions that promote the creation of wealth, as well as those that determine the distribution of wealth.

37. We believe it is the responsibility of every society to provide people with the means to live at a level consistent with their standing as persons created in the image of God.

Justice and poverty
38. Biblical justice means impartially rendering to everyone their due in conformity with the standards of God's moral law. Paul uses justice (or righteousness) in its most comprehensive sense as a metaphor to describe God's creative and powerful redemptive love. Christ, solely in grace, brought us, into God's commonwealth, who were strangers to it and because of sin cut off from it (Rom. 1:17–18; 3:21–26; Eph. 2:4–22). In Biblical passages which deal with the distribution of the benefits of social life in the context of social conflict and social wrong, justice is related particularly to what is due to groups such as the poor, widows, orphans, resident aliens, wage earners and slaves. The common link among these groups is powerlessness by virtue of economic and social needs. The justice called forth is to restore these groups to the provision God intends for them. God's law expresses this justice and indicates its demands. Further, God's intention is for people to live, not in isolation, but in society. The poor are described as those who are weak with respect to the rest of the community; the responsibility of the community is stated as "to make them strong" so that they can continue to take their place in the community (Lev. 25:35–36). One of the dilemmas of the poor is their loss of community (Job 22:5; Ps. 107:4–9, 33–36). Indeed their various needs are those that tend to prevent people from being secure and contributing members of society. One essential characteristic of Biblical justice is the meeting of basic needs that have been denied in contradiction to the standards of scripture; but further, the Bible gives indication of how to identify which needs

are basic. They are those essential, not just for life, but for life in society.

39. Justice requires special attention to the weak members of the community because of their greater vulnerability. In this sense, justice is partial. Nevertheless, the civil arrangements in rendering justice are not to go beyond what is due to the poor or to the rich (Deut. 1:17; Lev. 19:15). In this sense justice is ultimately impartial. Justice is so fundamental that it characterises the personal virtues and personal relationships of individuals as they faithfully follow God's standards. Those who violate God's standards, however, receive God's retributive justice, which often removes the offender from society or from the divine community.

40. Justice requires conditions such that each person is able to participate in society in a way compatible with human dignity. Absolute poverty, where people lack even minimal food and housing, basic education, health care, and employment, denies people the basic economic resources necessary for just participation in the community. Corrective action with and on behalf of the poor is a necessary act of justice. This entails responsibilities for individuals, families, churches, and governments.

41. Justice may also require socio-political actions that enable the poor to help themselves and be the subjects of their own development and the development of their communities. We believe that we and the institutions in which we participate are responsible to create an environment of law, economic activity, and spiritual nurture which creates these conditions.

Some urgent contemporary issues
42. Inequitable international economic relations aggravate poverty in poor countries. Many of these countries suffer under a burden of debt service which could only be repaid at an unacceptable price to the poor, unless there is a radical restructuring both of national economic policies and international economic relations. The combination of increasing interest rates and falling commodity prices in the early 1980s has increased this debt service burden. Both lenders

and borrowers shared in creating this debt. The result has been increasing impoverishment of the people. Both lenders and borrowers must share responsibility for finding solutions. We urgently encourage governments and international financial institutions to redouble their efforts to find ways to reduce the international indebtedness of the Third World, and to ensure the flow of both private and public productive capital where appropriate.

43. Government barriers to the flow of goods and services often work to the disadvantage of the poor. We particularly abhor the protectionist policies of the wealthy nations which are detrimental to developing countries. Greater freedom and trade between nations is an important part of reducing poverty worldwide.

44. Justice requires that the value of money be reliably known and stable, thus inflation represents poor stewardship and defrauds the nations' citizens. It wastes resources and is particularly harmful to the poor and the powerless. The wealthier members of society find it much easier to protect themselves against inflation than do the poor. Rapid changes in prices drastically affect the ability of the poor to purchase basic goods.

45. Annual global military expenditures equal the annual income of the poorest one-half of the world's people. These vast, excessive military expenditures detract from the task of meeting basic human needs, such as food, health care, and education. We are encouraged by the possibilities represented by the changes in the USSR and Eastern Europe, and improving relations between East and West. We urge that a major part of the resulting "peace dividend" be used to provide sustainable solutions to the problems of the world's poor.

46. Drug use and trafficking destroys both rich and poor nations. Drug consumption reflects spiritual poverty among the people and societies in which drug use is apparent. Drug trafficking undermines the national economies of those who produce drugs. The economic, social, and spiritual costs of drug use are unacceptable. The two key agents involved in this problem must change: the rich markets which consume drugs and the poorer countries which produce

them. Therefore both must work urgently to find solutions. The rich markets which consume drugs must end their demand. And the poorer countries which produce them must switch to other products.

47. We deplore economic systems based on policies, laws and regulations whose effect is to favour privileged minorities and to exclude the poor from fully legitimate activities. Such systems are not only inefficient, but are immoral as well in that participating in and benefitting from the formal economy depends on conferred privilege of those who have access and influence to public and private institutions rather than on inventiveness and hard work. Actions need to be taken by public and private institutions to reduce and simplify the requirements and costs of participating in the national economy.

48. There is abundant evidence that investment in small scale enterprises run by and for the poor can have a positive impact upon income and job creation for the poor. Contrary to the myths upheld by traditional financial institutions, the poor are often good entrepreneurs and excellent credit risks. We deplore the lack of credit available to the poor in the informal sector. We strongly encourage governments, financial institutions, and Non Governmental Organisations to redouble their efforts to significantly increase credit to the poor. We feel so strongly about this that a separate statement dedicated to credit-based, income generation programs has been issued by the conference.

D. FREEDOM, GOVERNMENT AND ECONOMICS

49. With the United Nations Declaration of Human Rights, the language of human rights has become pervasive throughout the world. It expresses the urgent plight of suffering people whose humanity is daily being denied them by their oppressors. In some cases rights language has been misused by those who claim that anything they want is theirs "by right". This breadth of application has led some to reject rights as a concept, stating that if everything becomes a right then nothing will be a right, since all rights imply corresponding responsibilities. Therefore it is important to have clear criteria for what defines rights.

Christian distinctives
50. All human interaction is judged by God and is accountable to God. In seeking human rights we search for an authority or norm which transcends our situation. God is that authority; God's character constitutes that norm. Since human rights are a priori rights, they are not conferred by the society or the state. Rather, human rights are rooted in the fact that every human being is made in the image of God. The deepest ground of human dignity is that while we were yet sinners, Christ died for us (Rom. 5:8).

51. In affirmation of the dignity of God's creatures, God's justice for them requires life, freedom, and sustenance. The divine requirements of justice establish corresponding rights for human beings to whom justice is due. The right to life is the most basic human right. God created human beings as free moral agents. As such, they have the right to freedom—e.g., freedom of religion, speech, and assembly. Their freedom, however, is properly used only in dependence on God. It is a requirement of justice that human beings, including refugees and stateless persons, are able to live in society with dignity. Human beings therefore have a claim on other human beings for social arrangements that ensure that they have access to the sustenance that makes life in society possible.

52. The fact that in becoming Christians we may choose to forego our rights out of love for others and in trust of God's providential

care does not mean that such rights cease to exist. Christians may endure the violation of their rights with great courage but work vigorously for the identical rights of others in similar circumstances. However it may not be appropriate to do so in some circumstances. Indeed this disparity between Christian contentment and campaigning on behalf of others in adverse situations is a witness to the work and love of God.

53. All of us share the same aspirations as human beings to have our rights protected—whether the right to life, freedom, or sustenance. Yet the fact of sin and the conflict of competing human rights means that our aspirations are never completely fulfilled in this life. Through Christ, sin and evil have been conquered. They will remain a destructive force until the consummation of all things. But that in no way reduces our horror at the widespread violation of human rights today.

Democracy

54. As a model, modern political democracy is characterised by limited government of a temporary character, by the division of power within the government, the distinction between state and society, pluralism, the rule of law, institutionalisation of freedom rights (including free and regular elections), and a significant amount of non-governmental control of property. We recognise that no political system is directly prescribed by scripture, but we believe that biblical values and historical experience call Christians to work for the adequate participation of all people in the decision-making processes on questions that affect their lives.

55. We also recognise that simply to vote periodically is not a sufficient expression of democracy. For a society to be truly democratic economic power must be shared widely and class and status distinctions must not be barriers preventing access to economic and social institutions. Democracies are also open to abuse through the very channels which make them democratic. Small, economically powerful groups sometimes dominate the political process. Democratic majorities can be swayed by materialistic, racist, or nationalistic sentiments to engage in unjust policies. The fact that all human

institutions are fallen means that the people must be constantly alert to and critical of all that is wrong.

56. We recognise that no particular economic system is directly prescribed by scripture. Recent history suggests that a dispersion of ownership of the means of production is a significant component of democracy. Monopolistic ownership, either by the state, large economic institutions, or oligarchies is dangerous. Widespread ownership, either in a market economy or a mixed system tends to decentralise power and prevent totalitarianism.

The concentration of economic power
57. Economic power can be concentrated in the hands of a few people in a market economy. When that occurs political decisions tend to be made for economic reasons and the average member of society is politically and economically marginalised. Control over economic life may thus be far removed from a large part of the population. Transnational corporations can also wield enormous influence on some economies. Despite these problems, economic power is diffused within market-oriented economies to a greater extent than in other systems.

58. In centrally planned economies, economic decisions are made for political reasons, people's economic choices are curtailed, and the economy falters. Heavy state involvement and regulation within market economies can also result in concentrations of power that effectively marginalise poorer members of the society. Corruption almost inevitably follows from concentrated economic power. Widespread corruption so undermines society that there is a virtual breakdown of legitimate order.

Capitalism and culture
59. As non-capitalist countries increasingly turn away from central planning and toward the market, the question of capitalism's effect on culture assumes more and more importance. The market system can be an effective means of economic growth, but can, in the process, cause people to think that ultimate meaning is found in the accumulation of more goods. The overwhelming consumerism of

Western societies is testimony to the fact that the material success of capitalism encourages forces and attitudes that are decidedly non-Christian. One such attitude is the treatment of workers as simply costs or productive inputs, without recognition of their humanity. There is also the danger that the model of the market, which may work well in economic transactions, will be assumed to be relevant to other areas of life, and people may consequently believe that what the market encourages is therefore best or most true.

The role of government

60. Government is designed to serve the purposes of God to foster community, particularly in response to our rebellious nature (Rom. 13:1, 4). As an institution administered by human beings, government can exacerbate problems of power, greed, and envy. However, it can, where properly constructed and constrained, serve to limit some of these sinful tendencies. Therefore, it is the responsibility of Christians to work for governmental structures that serve justice. Such structures must respect the principle that significant decisions about local human communities are usually best made at a level of government most directly responsible to the people affected.

61. At a minimum, government must establish a rule of law that protects life, secures freedom, and provides basic security. Special care must be taken to make sure the protection of fundamental rights is extended to all members of society, especially the poor and oppressed (Prov. 31:8–9; Dan. 4:27). Too often government institutions are captured by the economically or socially powerful. Thus, equality before the law fails to exist for those without power. Government must also have regard for economic efficiency and appropriately limit its own scope and action.

62. The provision of sustenance rights is also an appropriate function of government. Such rights must be carefully defined so that government's involvement will not encourage irresponsible behaviour and the breakdown of families and communities. In a healthy society, this fulfilment of rights will be provided through a diversity of institutions so that the government's role will be that of last resort.

Mediating structures

63. One of the phenomena associated with the modern world is the increasing divide between private and public sectors. The need for a bridge between these two sectors has led to an emphasis on mediating institutions. The neighbourhood, the family, the church and other voluntary associations are all such institutions. As the early church did in its context, these institutions provide citizens with many opportunities for participation and leadership. They also provide other opportunities for loyalty in addition to the state and the family. Their role in meeting the needs of members of the community decreases the need for centralised government. They also provide a channel for individuals to influence government, business, and other large institutions. Therefore Christians should encourage governments everywhere to foster vigorous voluntary associations.

64. The future of poverty alleviation is likely to involve expanded microeconomic income generation programs and entrepreneurial development of the so-called "informal sector" as it becomes part of the transformed formal economy. In this context, there will most likely be an even greater role for Non Governmental Organizations. In particular, church bodies will be able to make a significant and creative contribution in partnership with the poor, acting as mediating institutions by virtue of the churches' longstanding grassroots involvement in local communities.

Conclusion

65. As we conclude, we thank God for the opportunity God has given us to participate in this conference. Through our time together we have been challenged to express our faith in the area of economic life in practical ways. We acknowledge that all too often we have allowed society to shape our views and actions and have failed to apply scriptural teaching in this crucial area of our lives, and we repent.

We now encourage one another to uphold Christian economic values in the face of unjust and subhuman circumstances. We realise, however, that ethical demands are often ineffective because they are reinforced only by individual conscience and that the proclamation of Christian values needs to be accompanied by action to encourage institutional and structural changes which would foster these values in our communities. We will therefore endeavour to seek every opportunity to work for the implementation of the principles outlined in this **Declaration**, in faithfulness to God's calling.

We urge all people, and especially Christians, to adopt stewardship and justice as the guiding principles for all aspects of economic life, particularly for the sake of those who are most vulnerable. These principles must be applied in all spheres of life. They have to do with our use of material resources and lifestyle as well as with the way people and nations relate to one another. With girded loins and burning lamps we wait for the return of our Lord Jesus Christ when justice and peace shall embrace.

FACTS RELATED TO U.S. WEALTH FROM A GLOBAL CHRISTIAN PERSPECTIVE

John and Sylvia Ronsvalle

The Bible encourages believers to look at the big picture. But global realities—the size of the evangelistic task, the enormity of famine and poverty—should not intimidate us, for Scripture also offers a high view of the believer. The same God who charges his followers to "go and make disciples of *all* nations" provides the means to fulfill his tasks and shows confidence in the courage and resourcefulness of his messengers.

As new creations, with minds renewed by the Holy Spirit, we can explore what it means to be disciples as U.S. citizens at this particular point in history. Although Christians are daily bombarded, cajoled, and tantalized by our consumption-oriented culture, the discriminating disciple can gain a clear perspective on the challenges facing the church in the United States. To the extent that believers have a valid overview of how well the church is meeting its mission, there is a solid basis for making informed choices about life's big-ticket decisions.

The nine facts that follow are selected from an abundance of information; but together with the graphs and thought questions provided, these few bits of data can help church members develop a strategic view of the world.

Strategic data often come to us in large numbers. It is difficult to think about a billion dollars. Yet simple comparisons can help. For example, one statistic that stands out is that U.S. Protestants spent $1.7 billion on overseas ministries in 1987 (see Fact 5). One can gain a sense of how small this seemingly large number is when it is compared to the $12 billion U.S. consumers spent on candy alone in 1988. With such an understanding, we can better set our priorities so as to be faithful in these exciting times.

Fact 1: Americans were approximately 200% richer in 1985 than in 1933—the depth of the Great Depression. Yet, Protestants gave a smaller portion of their income to their churches in 1985 than in 1933.

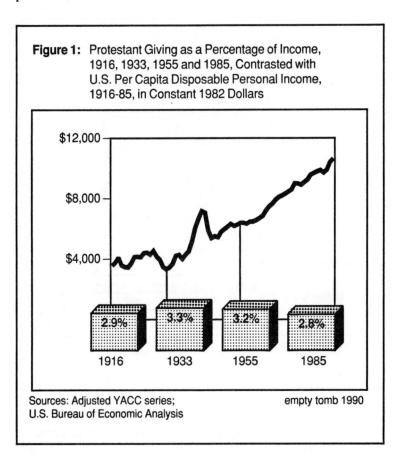

Figure 1: Protestant Giving as a Percentage of Income, 1916, 1933, 1955 and 1985, Contrasted with U.S. Per Capita Disposable Personal Income, 1916-85, in Constant 1982 Dollars

Sources: Adjusted YACC series;   empty tomb 1990
U.S. Bureau of Economic Analysis

Question 1: Is there something about suffering that makes people more generous? Are you more or less generous when you are experiencing difficult times?

Fact 2: A national survey showed that people with lower incomes gave more of their income to religion than those with higher incomes.

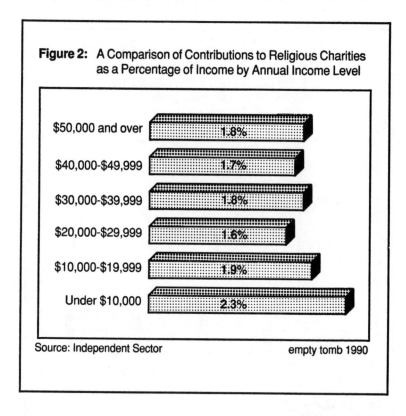

Figure 2: A Comparison of Contributions to Religious Charities as a Percentage of Income by Annual Income Level

$50,000 and over — 1.8%
$40,000-$49,999 — 1.7%
$30,000-$39,999 — 1.8%
$20,000-$29,999 — 1.6%
$10,000-$19,999 — 1.9%
Under $10,000 — 2.3%

Source: Independent Sector   empty tomb 1990

Question 2: What might be the reasons that lower-income people give more of their income to religion than economically better-off people do?

Fact 3: Research has shown that people become increasingly generous in giving to religion as they grow older.

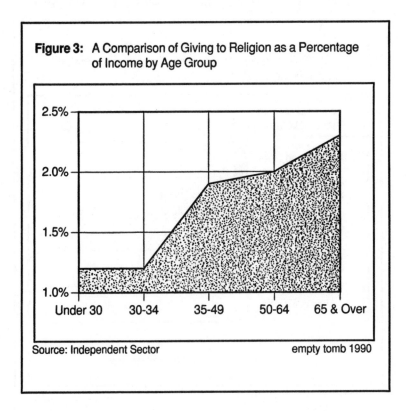

Figure 3: A Comparison of Giving to Religion as a Percentage of Income by Age Group

Source: Independent Sector

empty tomb 1990

Question 3: What factors might influence the level of giving by different age groups?

Fact 4: Americans pay billions of dollars each year in credit-card interest payments. In 1986, for example, 26.98 million taxpayers listed on their itemized returns the amount of credit-card interest they paid. Although the average interest payment was $535, the combined total was $14.43 billion.

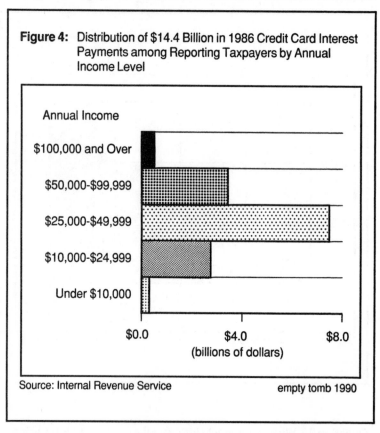

Figure 4: Distribution of $14.4 Billion in 1986 Credit Card Interest Payments among Reporting Taxpayers by Annual Income Level

Annual Income

$100,000 and Over

$50,000-$99,999

$25,000-$49,999

$10,000-$24,999

Under $10,000

$0.0 $4.0 $8.0
(billions of dollars)

Source: Internal Revenue Service   empty tomb 1990

Question 4: Were interest charges on credit cards an expense for you in the past twelve months? By planning purchases differently, are there activities you could undertake with the money saved to make an impact on world need, such as sponsoring a child, supporting a local shelter for the homeless or food pantry, or increasing your gift to your church missions budget?

Fact 5: The expenditures for U.S. Protestant overseas ministries in 1987 totaled $1.7 billion. This amount includes denominational programs (Southern Baptists and the Assemblies of God being two of the largest); interdenominational efforts of the National Association of Evangelicals and the National Council of the Churches of Christ in the U.S.A.; and non-denominational groups such as World Vision.

Figure 5: A Comparison of the 1987 Protestant Overseas Ministries Budget with Selected 1987 and 1988 Annual U.S. Consumer Expenditures

Protestant overseas ministries	$1.7 billion
New golf equipment	$2.0 billion
Chewing gum	$2.5 billion
Pinball machines	$2.6 billion
Skin care	$2.7 billion
Arcade video games	$2.9 billion
Women's sheer hosiery	$3.5 billion
Candy[*]	$12.0 billion
Diet-related products and services[*]	$29.0 billion

Sources: MARC; Associated Press; Newsweek; USA Today
*1988 Expenditures

empty tomb 1990

Question 5: What "optional" purchases do you regularly make? How does the amount you spend on these purchases compare to the amount you contribute annually to missions?

Fact 6: Although a number of formerly "closed" societies have begun to permit the printing and distribution of Bibles, the necessary resources have not grown as rapidly as the opportunities. For example, the United Bible Societies have received requests for millions of Bibles from Christians in the USSR and Eastern Europe which they cannot fill.

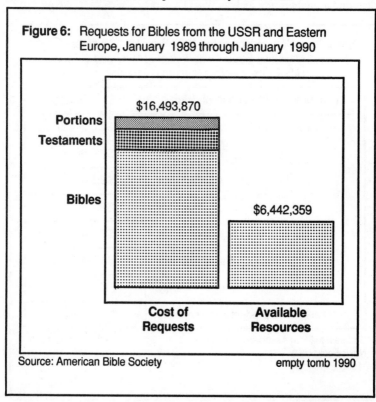

Figure 6: Requests for Bibles from the USSR and Eastern Europe, January 1989 through January 1990

$16,493,870

Portions
Testaments

Bibles

$6,442,359

Cost of
Requests

Available
Resources

Source: American Bible Society   empty tomb 1990

(The demand for Bibles worldwide is great. It costs three dollars on the average for a Bible to be printed and distributed anywhere around the globe. The American Bible Society has a Bible-a-Month Club that allows individuals to pay for the printing and distribution of a Bible in another country on a regular basis.)

Question 6: Do the mission activities supported by your congregation include the distribution and printing of Bibles somewhere in the world?

Fact 7: A recent study found that children in the U.S. aged 4 to 12 have an estimated $7.2 billion a year to spend. They receive allowances, earn money by doing household tasks or other jobs, and receive money as gifts.

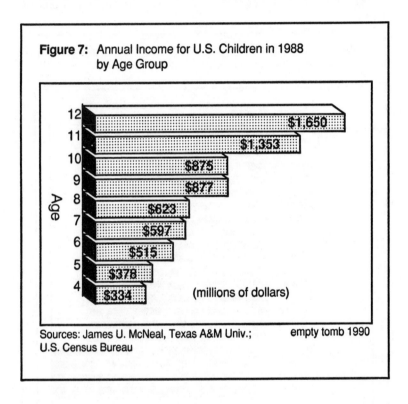

Figure 7: Annual Income for U.S. Children in 1988 by Age Group

(millions of dollars)

Sources: James U. McNeal, Texas A&M Univ.; U.S. Census Bureau

empty tomb 1990

Question 7: How are children in your congregation being encouraged to investigate what stewardship means?

Fact 8: Domestic poverty continues to be a problem in the U.S. The U.S. has a high infant-mortality rate compared to other developed nations. This fact is due, at least in part, to pockets of poverty within the U.S. Chicago, for example, has an infant-mortality rate equal to that of Cuba and Bulgaria—that is, 15 deaths of children under age one for every 1,000 live births.

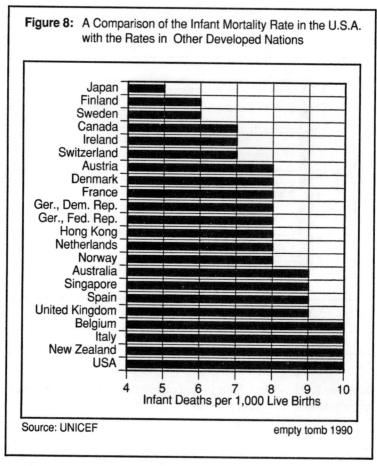

Figure 8: A Comparison of the Infant Mortality Rate in the U.S.A. with the Rates in Other Developed Nations

Source: UNICEF

empty tomb 1990

Question 8: What channels of service are available to you through you church or a ministry in your community to assist low-income neighbors?

Fact 9:   In the past decade, the number of children under age five who have died from preventable poverty conditions around the globe is greater than the number of people who have been killed in all the 471 wars between 1700 and 1987.

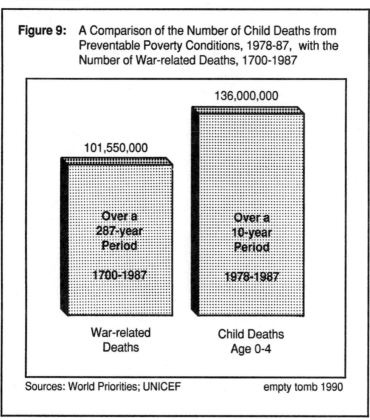

Figure 9:   A Comparison of the Number of Child Deaths from Preventable Poverty Conditions, 1978-87, with the Number of War-related Deaths, 1700-1987

136,000,000

101,550,000

Over a 287-year Period 1700-1987

Over a 10-year Period 1978-1987

War-related Deaths

Child Deaths Age 0-4

Sources: World Priorities; UNICEF   empty tomb 1990

(The annual child-death rate has actually decreased since the 1950s, although progress has slowed recently. Demographic studies indicate that societies do not lower their birth rate until the child-death rate declines— when the child-death rate declines, the birth rate begins to drop even faster.)

Question 9:   What verses give us guidance regarding our response to parents facing the death of their children from poverty conditions around the globe? What specific actions can you take through your congregation to help stop children from dying in at least one area of the world?

ABOUT THE AUTHORS

Ted W. Engstrom *is president emeritus of World Vision, Monrovia, California. He is a member of the boards of African Enterprise, Azusa Pacific University, Dynacom Ministries, Focus on the Family, the Christian Ministries Management Association, and several other evangelical ministries. He has written forty books, including* The Making of a Christian Leader *(Zondervan, 1976) and* The Art of Management for Christian Leaders *(Zondervan, 1989).*

W. Ward Gasque *is provost of Eastern College in St. Davids, Pennsylvania. He is also professor-at-large at Regent College, Vancouver, British Columbia, where he served as a founding faculty member. He is a graduate of Wheaton College, Fuller Theological Seminary, and Manchester University, England. He has written numerous articles and lectured widely throughout the United States and around the world. He is the editor of* The New International Biblical Commentary *(Hendrickson). He coedited, with Carl E. Armerding,* A Guide to Biblical Prophecy *(Hendrickson, 1989).*

Wayne A. Grudem *is associate professor of biblical and systematic theology at Trinity Evangelical Divinity School, Deerfield, Illinois. He is a graduate of Harvard University, Westminster Theological Seminary, and the University of Cambridge, England, writing his doctoral dissertation on the gift of prophecy in 1 Corinthians. He is the author of* The Gift of Prophecy in the New Testament and Today *(Crossway Books, 1988), and* 1 Peter *in the Tyndale New Testament Commentary series (Eerdmans, 1988).*

Karen Halvorsen *is a free-lance writer. She is a graduate of the State University of New York–Binghamton and Wheaton College. She has written several magazine articles, including* Christian History *magazine.*

Timothy K. Jones *is assistant editor of* CHRISTIANITY TODAY. *He is a graduate of Pepperdine University and Princeton Theological Seminary, and is an ordained minister in the Church of the Brethren. He is the author of the soon-to-be-released* Mentor and Friend *(Lion, 1991).*

Kenneth S. Kantzer *is distinguished professor of biblical and systematic theology and dean emeritus of Trinity Evangelical Divinity School, and chancellor of Trinity College, Deerfield, Illinois. A former editor of* CHRISTIANITY TODAY, *he serves as a senior editor of that magazine and dean of the Christianity Today Institute. Kantzer is a graduate of Ashland College, Ohio State University, Faith Theological Seminary, and Harvard University, from which he received his Ph.D. His publications include chapters in* Religions in a Changing World, The Evangelicals, *and* Jesus of Nazareth: Savior and Lord.

Pedrito U. Maynard-Reid *is lecturer of New Testament, Walla Walla College, College Place, Washington. He received his Th.D. from Andrews University. He has written* Poverty and Wealth in James *(Orbis, 1987).*

David Neff *is senior associate editor of* CHRISTIANITY TODAY. *He is a graduate of Loma Linda University and Andrews University, and he has pursued additional graduate study at San Francisco Theological Seminary. Before coming to* CHRISTIANITY TODAY, *he served as editor of* HIS, *InterVarsity Christian Fellowship's erstwhile magazine for college students.*

John Ronsvalle, *Ph.D., received degrees from Syracuse University, Fuller Theological Seminary, and the University of Illinois. Together with his wife,* **Sylvia Ronsvalle,** *a graduate of the University of Illinois, he founded and administers* empty tomb, inc., *a Christian research and service organization. The Ronsvalles, having coauthored a book, and a national study and various articles on church-giving trends in the United States, are currently developing The National Money for Missions Program, a stewardship enhancement project.*

Thomas E. Schmidt *is associate professor of religious studies at Westmont College in Santa Barbara, California. He earned his Ph.D.*

from Cambridge University and is the author of Hostility to Wealth in the Synoptic Gospels *(Sheffield Academic Press, 1987).*

Tom Sine *is a Christian futurist and convener of the Creative Futures Center in Seattle, a group that helps denominations and Christian groups to anticipate more effectively tomorrow's challenges and to respond more creatively to those growing needs. Sine is a graduate of the University of Washington, where he earned his Ph.D. in history. He has written* The Mustard Seed Conspiracy *(Word, 1981),* Why Settle for More and Miss the Best *(Word, 1988), and* Wild Hope *(Word, 1990).*

Raymond C. Van Leeuwen *is professor of religion and theology at Calvin College in Grand Rapids, Michigan. He earned his Ph.D. from the University of Saint Michaels College in Toronto, and is an ordained pastor in the Christian Reformed Church. He is the author of* Context and Meaning in Proverbs 25–27 *(Scholars Press, 1988).*

J. Isamu Yamamoto *is book editor for* CHRISTIANITY TODAY. *He is a graduate of Gordon-Conwell Theological Seminary. He has written* The Puppet Master: An Inquiry into Sun Myung Moon and the Unification Church *(1977) and* Beyond Buddhism: A Basic Introduction to the Buddhist Tradition *(1982), both published by InterVarsity Press.*